RHODESIA
THE STRUGGLE FOR FREEDOM

ORBIS BOOKS
MARYKNOLL NEW YORK

RHODESIA
THE STRUGGLE
FOR FREEDOM

LEONARD T. KAPUNGU

TO THE PEOPLE OF ZIMBABWE

Nothing should divide patriots
when the nation is in danger,
when the honor of the motherland lies trampled
by an immigrant minority group.

Library of Congress Catalog Card Number: 74-76966.
ISBN: 0-88344-435-6.

Manufactured in the United States of America.

The views herein expressed are those of the author, and do not necessarily reflect those of the publisher or any member of the Maryknoll community.

Contents

Foreword

Approximately 5,525,000 human beings live in the land of Zimbabwe.[1] 5,250,000 of these people are Africans, 250,000 are European settlers, and 25,000 are Asians and peoples of mixed origins. The social, political, and economic rights due to all human beings are reserved only for the 250,000 European settlers. The best motives of the nineteenth century colonial expansion movement—namely, exploration, altruism, and a misguided sense of being emissaries of "Christianity, commerce, and civilization"—have, in the late twentieth century, degenerated into the worst aspects of Social Darwinism: racial prejudice and paternalism, economic greed, an arrogant closedmindedness to the reality of the times, and the unjust use of force to accomplish one's ends.

On November 11, 1965, Ian Smith's Rhodesian government declared its unilateral declaration of independence (UDI) from Great Britain in order to ward off British political pressure to ensure eventual democratic majority rule in Zimbabwe. When reading the Rhodesian UDI, citizens of the United States will be quick to note the intended similarity with America's Declaration of Independence, as well as, I hope, the omission of key passages which state that all men are created equal, are endowed with inalienable human rights, and, most importantly, that governments derive their just powers from the consent of the governed.

Because the Africans in Zimbabwe are denied their inalienable rights, there is no majority approval for the white minority regime. Lord Pearce's Commission in May 1972 was forced to report to the British Parliament that the African population under the leadership of the African National Council unanimously rejected any British-Rhodesian accord which did not guarantee specific programs to implement majority rule in the near future.

Majority rule is a sensitive issue to European settlers in Rhodesia. The white population is only 5 percent of the total. If the blacks refer to their European rulers as "settlers," they are speaking the literal truth about a group of foreign-born people who have come to Rhodesia to assume control of the land and its people. Three-fourths of the white population have been in the country less than twenty-five years—a post-World War II immigration; one-fourth of the white population has been there less than ten years; one-third has migrated northward from South Africa.

Men and women of conscience in Rhodesia and outside have condemned the unilateral declaration of independence and the racist policies of the Rhodesian regime. The churches in Rhodesia, after a long period of silence and what has appeared to the Africans as connivance with the Rhodesian regimes, have found the policies of the Ian Smith regime "irreconcilable with God's law and in time to come [they] must have the most tragic consequences for the country."

Despite all these warnings the Rhodesian regime has continued with deliberate policies intended to ensure the permanent domination of the white population over the African majority. Further, this racist regime has found sympathy in some capitals of the world that profess their adherence to democratic principles.

What does all this mean for readers in the United States? We are only gradually recognizing that the United States foreign policy toward Southern Africa is one of weak lamentations concerning justice and purposeful laissez-faire with regard to international business interests. Some people of conscience in the United States, including both the Catholic and some Protestant churches, have issued statements urging the U.S. government to cut off all military cooperation with the white minority regimes in Southern Africa and to exert the strongest possible influence to effect racial equality in those areas; all private organizations with conscience responsible for investment funds have been asked to use their influence to bring about reforms in South Africa, Rhodesia, and Portuguese Africa. Men and women of conscience have also been reminded that they have an obligation to exert their influence for justice not only in the business field but also among political leaders and government officials and among the media. This was a small step—almost nothing in the mass-media milieu of the United States.

One must begin with a position of conscience based on knowledge. It is here that Dr. Kapungu's book will serve the reader well. Kapungu is a man of the soil of Zimbabwe, a descendant of the Shona people who controlled the interior gold trade routes ten centuries ago. He knows first hand the strength of African family life and African society. He has grown up under the various Rhodesian governments and been educated with different European missionary groups. The sufferings of his people are his own. His experience of being a ward in his own homeland at the hands of a white minority regime has left him acutely aware of the evils of oppression.

Leonard Kapungu received a doctoral education in Political Science at the University of London. He has been assistant professor of Political Science at the University of Maryland, a research fellow at the United Nations Institute for Training and Research, and has published a number of works on the tragedy of Southern Africa. He is intimately aware of the foibles of the British and American political scenes and the strengths and weaknesses of the Zimbabweans' own struggle for freedom. In a word, he is a man most qualified in honesty and knowledge to portray the story of Zimbabwe. His work reflects all the human goodness, suffering, determination, and courage that he and his countrymen bring to the cause of Zimbabwe.

Joseph P. Carney, M.M.
Associate Professor of African Studies

Maryknoll Seminary

---

[1]*Zimbabwe* is the name of the ancient ruins of a great acropolis located north of the Limpopo river. Its magnificent stone structures were situated in a commanding position along the gold trade route from the interior to the Indian Ocean during the eleventh to fifteenth centuries. Some of its construction has been estimated to have taken place as early as the eighth century, and the design and scope of the whole acropolis reflect a flourishing civilization. "Rhodesia" has an internationally recognized name because of the adventures of Cecil Rhodes in the 1890's, but all Africans look forward to the day when the name of their land between the Limpopo and Zambezi rivers—Zimbabwe—will reflect the dignity and heritage of more than twelve centuries.

CHAPTER 1

The Roots of Confrontation

Rhodesia is destined for a bloody confrontation between the white settlers, who exclusively enjoy political and economic power, and the Africans, the indigenous people of the land, who for more than eighty years have seen all their basic rights eroded. Such a confrontation is inevitable and is rooted in factors which we will categorize as (1) historical, (2) racial, (3) economic, (4) educational, and (5) political.

Historical Factors

Most historians who have studied the history of Rhodesia agree that about the end of first millennium A.D., food-producing people of the Iron Age moved southward towards central Africa.[1] Anthropologists have concluded that these people, whom they have classified as "BI," spoke a common language of Bantu syntax. These people have been identified as the Mashona who settled south of the Zambezi River.[2] Dr. Stanlake Samkange, an eminent historian from Zimbabwe and currently a professor at Harvard University, has concluded that "from about the end of the first millennium to the 1830's this area [south of the Zambezi River] was completely dominated by the Mashona."[3] Many other historians, including T.O. Ranger and D.P. Abraham, agree with this conclusion.

In the 1830's there were what Dr. Samkange calls "stirrings" to the south of the area inhabited by the Mashona. A group of the Zulu, who were engaged in these "stirrings," fled northwards and settled north of the Limpopo River. These new arrivals called themselves the Matebele. Thus, the area that lies between fifteen and twenty-three degrees south latitude and twenty-five and thirty-four degrees east longitude, bordered on the north by the Zambezi River and on the south by the Limpopo River, became a home of two peoples, the Mashona and the Matebele.

In the 1880's Cecil John Rhodes, an Englishman who had gone to South Africa to escape the cold weather of the British Isles, acquired a great deal of wealth from his dealings in diamonds. He became a millionaire and was full of passion and zeal to use his wealth in the expansion of the British Empire. He dreamed of seeing the British flag flying all over Africa from Cape Town in the south to Cairo in the north. Rhodes knew that a number of white people, like Piet Grobler and E. Lippert, were trying to persuade Lobengula, the king of the Matebele, to sign treaties with them. The king's armies had ravaged the whole area occupied by the Mashona in the attempt to establish his control. Grobler was a South African Boer [white of Dutch descent] and Lippert was a German. Rhodes dispatched a missionary, who was supposed to be a trusted friend of Lobengula, to persuade him to sign a treaty with the British. The missionary, Rev. John Moffat, persuaded the unsuspecting king to sign a treaty of friendship with Britain in February 1888. The treaty reads in part:

> It is hereby further agreed by Lobengula, Chief, in and over the Amandebele country with its dependencies as aforesaid, on behalf of himself and people, that he will refrain from entering into any correspondence or treaty with a Foreign State, or Power . . . . [4]

Rhodes and Moffat were seeking to prevent any other white power from entering into dealings with Lobengula. Since the king was illiterate, Moffat served as both the broker and the interpreter of the treaty to Lobengula. Lobengula was invited to sign the treaty by placing the letter X at the end of the document.

Rhodes moved fast in trying to gain more concessions from the king. Immediately after the Moffat treaty had been signed, he dispatched emissaries under the leadership of Charles Dunnell Rudd to join Moffat in Matebeleland and pressure the king to sign a mineral concession. Moffat himself attested to this pressure. He reported, "There are quite a number of whites present, and Lobengula does not know where to turn."[5] The king's African advisers were bribed, his white friends and advisers were dishonest, and promises which could not be fulfilled were made to him. But Lobengula hesitated. It is said he signed the Rudd Concession only after Rev. C.D. Helm, "on whom Lobengula relied for impartial advice since he believed the missionary to have the true interest of the Matebele at heart, advised Lobengula to grant concessions to the largest group—that of Rhodes. What the king did not know was that Helm was himself in Rhodes' pay."[6]

In the Rudd Concession Rhodes promised to pay Lobengula's "heirs and successors the sum of one hundred pounds sterling, British currency, on the first day of every lunar month," and to deliver to Lobengula one thousand Martini-Henry breech rifles, together with one hundred thousand rounds of ammunition, and further to deliver on the Zambezi River an armed steamboat. In return Rhodes was granted "the complete and exclusive charge over all metals and minerals" in the lands under Lobengula's control.[7]

It was this Rudd Concession that the white man used to move into Rhodesia. The concession is a highly technical document, couched in legalistic, contractual language. The illiterate king again signed with an X. Moffat and Helm, who were supposed to interpret the document to the king, had interests which were by no means congruent with the king's. As Samkange shows, the whole negotiation process of the Rudd Concession was clouded with trickery which casts doubt on whether Lobengula actually signed the concession. On some documents Lobengula used an elephant seal rather than an X. Such a seal was used on his letter calling for investigation of the Rudd Concession. The letter read:

> I hear it is published in the newspapers that I have granted a concession in all my country to Charles Dunnel Rudd, Rochfort Maguire and Francis Robert Thompson. As there is a great misunderstanding about this, all action in respect of the said concession is hereby suspended, pending an investigation to be made by me in my country.[8]

Why would Lobengula use the letter X and not the elephant seal on the Rudd Concession? He did use the elephant seal on a concession he granted Lippert. Noting that Rhodes was claiming that he had been granted mineral rights in the Rudd Concession, Lobengula proceeded to grant a land lease to Lippert for one hundred years. To make it authentic he signed the concession with the elephant seal. But Rhodes, realizing that the Lippert Concession could nullify his own concession, entered into a white-man-to-white-man deal with Lippert behind Lobengula's back. Lippert was to pay Lobengula $2,400, but he sold his concession to Rhodes for $3,000,000.

With the Rudd Concession in his hand Rhodes formed in 1889 the British South Africa Company (B.S.A.C.), under a royal charter from the British government. The charter granted the company power to exploit the mineral and agricultural wealth of Matebeleland and Mashonaland. In 1890 Rhodes picked his adventurers, and under the banner of his company and with the blessings of the British government they marched across the Limpopo River. Each of these adventurers was promised not less than fifteen gold claims [prospective gold mines] and a farm of 3,000 acres. On September 12, 1890, the adventurers, under the leadership of

Lieutenant Tyndale-Biscoe, arrived in what would later be Salisbury. They raised the Union Jack over their camp at a place that is now known as Cecil Square, the heart of Salisbury. With jubilation they named the country they were occupying "Rhodesia," in honor of Cecil John Rhodes.

The first European settlers were very suspicious and fearful of the Africans, whom they regarded as "stone-age savages." They resented the existence of Lobengula's kingdom and considered his standing armies a threat to their settlement. They looked for the most convenient moment and the slightest pretext to destroy this kingdom and build a white dominion in the name of Her Majesty, Queen Victoria of Great Britain. Lobengula, for his part, soon realized that Lippert and Rhodes had betrayed him. He saw the lands of his people being parcelled out and occupied by European settlers and his people being herded to work for them. What he had suspected all along now became very clear to him: The white men had no good intentions. Lobengula feared that if the white men were allowed to go unchallenged his days would be numbered.

Thus, from the very beginning the Europeans and the Africans regarded each other with suspicion, distrust, and hate. Each sought for ways to destroy the other and rejected any notion that they could coexist.

The first explosion came in 1893 when Lobengula mobilized his armies in an attempt to terminate European settlement. The Matebele War broke out between the white settlers and the Africans. Fierce battles raged, the spear against the machine gun. Historian T.O. Ranger notes, "the armies which shattered the Ndebele [Lobengula's] Monarchy in 1893 were deployments of white power on a scale unrivalled anywhere else in East and Central Africa."[9] The Africans fought with courage, annihilating the white settlers in the Shangaan Patrol, but they fell before the might of their foes. From then on the European settlers have argued that by their blood they conquered the Africans and established their ownership over the country. They say that by the defeat in the war of 1893, the Africans lost any right they may have had over their own country.

But the Africans, feeling that the land was theirs by right, despite trickery, fraud, and military defeat, seethed with deep hatred of the Europeans, who after 1893 were dispossessing them of their land with impunity. They looked forward to the day when justice would prevail. On March 24, 1896, the first white man since 1893 was killed, and soon after the whole country was in the grip of coordinated rebellion in both Mashonaland and Matebeleland. According to the settlers' own account as narrated by Ranger, "By the evening of March thirtieth not a white man was left alive in the outlying districts of Matebeleland. . . . Between these two dates many escaped or were brought into the laager [military defensive camp] by relief parties, but a large number, one hundred and forty-five in all, were treacherously murdered."[10] Ranger vividly describes the rebellion in Mashonaland: "The outbreak of the Shona rising in the third week of June 1896 is one of the great dramas of white Rhodesian history. Its total unexpectedness; its appalling impact upon a community most of whose fighting men were away in Matebeleland; the terror and courage of the isolated groups of settlers; all this gives a quality of true excitement and even grandeur to the many reminiscences which survive."[11] The memory of the events of 1896 stand very clear in the minds of the Europeans. Mrs. Nora S. Kane, daughter of an early Rhodesian settler, narrated the horrors of the rebellions and quotes a letter written by Mrs. Anne Fletcher to her relatives in South Africa. Mrs. Fletcher wrote:

> There lay the family of the Cunninghams—father, mother and six children, brutally murdered and chopped about with battle axes, and thrown into a heap outside. There were small children of about three or four simply cut to pieces . . . . [12]

The African wrath had struck back. Most white historians,

including Ranger, who claims to be sympathetic to the African cause in Rhodesia, have described the events of 1896 with a great deal of bias. They have tended to emphasize the "brutality" with which the Africans killed white settlers. But they seldom refer to the brutality with which the white settlers slaughtered the Africans. Stanlake Samkange has sought to redress this gap in the history of Rhodesia by presenting a full documentation of the atrocities committed by the Europeans from 1892 to 1896.[13] He narrates how a chief, his son, and "twenty-one other natives were killed" simply to "serve as a useful example" to the African people.[14] The perpetrator of these assassinations, Captain Charles Lendy, was rewarded with promotion to the position of magistrate. One white official, Dr. L. Jameson, said "impertinent natives" deserved to be shot, and he boasted that he could always find "good explanations" for slaughtering Africans.[15]

The events of the period between 1892 and 1896 left very bitter memories with both the Africans and the white settlers. The bitterness with which the rebellions of 1896 were fought and suppressed still clouds the relationship between the Europeans (in Rhodesia any white person is officially a European) and the Africans of today's Rhodesia. To the Rhodesian Europeans the past is still part of the present. The Rhodesian European child grows up conscious of the horrors of the early days. At school and at home he reads of the Last Stand of the Shangaan Patrol. In his books he sees Captain Spreakly with his laager in the Market Square in Bulawayo. As he rides along the streets of Salisbury with his parents he reads the names of his heroes in the streets: Rhodes Avenue, Jameson Avenue, Victoria Street, Pioneer Street. At the center of Salisbury and Bulawayo, the two largest cities of Rhodesia, he beholds the elegant statue of Rhodes, whom Sandy Tullock, an early settler, described in his diary as "our Moses and our law-giver." In July every Rhodesian European celebrates the Rhodes and Founder's Days. Every year on September 12 Europeans commemorate Occupation Day, or as it is now called, Pioneer Day. They join government officials in laying wreaths at the statue of Rhodes. In Gwelo, the fourth largest city of Rhodesia, Europeans honor public memorials dedicated to settlers "murdered by natives." The Rhodesian European child has never been allowed to escape the past. He lives with it. It is part of him and he grows up with the prejudices born out of the sufferings of the past so distant from him.

The African child also grows up with deep hatred of the European in Rhodesia. To him the European represents dispossession of his land, violation of his dignity as a person, and denial of his aspirations. He knows from stories told by grandparents by the fireside that force and deception were employed to subjugate him. Samkange observes:

> The Mashona were subjected to what is still remembered even today as "Charter Ro" (Charter Law)—rough and brutal treatment. This and the sjambok [leather whip] have become part of Mashona oral tradition, so much so that when one roughs up and subjects a man to particularly unfair and brutal violence the Mashona say "Wayita Chata ro"—"he has practiced Charter Company Justice."[16]

The stories of these injustices have been passed from one generation to another just as the white settlers have used school books to instill in their children the bitterness of the past.

In the history of Rhodesia lie the roots of the confrontation of the future. The African National Council, formed in December 1971 to spearhead the African struggle in Rhodesia, noted that its members were "heirs to the People's Struggle which has ceaselessly been waged since the imposition of alien rule in 1890."[17] Time has not made either the Europeans or the Africans forget the past.

Racial Factors

The whole fabric on which the Rhodesian social structure was founded is made up of the belief that the white race is superior to the black. In fact, Cecil John Rhodes himself strongly believed that the English "race" was the best in the world. He once asked his fellow Englishmen, "Have you ever thought how lucky you are to be born an Englishman when there were so many millions who were not?"[18] He also said, "We are the finest race in the world and the more of the world we inhabit the better it is for the human race."[19] When the atrocities his adventurers in Rhodesia were committing against the Africans were brought to his attention, he explained, "I prefer land to niggers."[20]

Such was the founding father of white Rhodesia—an acknowledged racist. His successors have carried on his philosophy and have implemented it. Most of the administrators and prime ministers of Rhodesia right down to Ian Douglas Smith have been racists. Marshall Hole, an administrator of the British South Africa Company in the 1890's, regarded the Africans as savages because they did not know "the different uses of the multitude of strange utensils."[21] Godfrey Huggins, later Lord Malvern, the Prime Minister of Rhodesia from 1933 to 1953 and the first Prime Minister of the Federation of Rhodesia and Nyasaland from 1953 to 1956, told the Oxford Union:

> Even in such a vast continent as Africa it seems unlikely that the Africans were not touched by some of the ancient civilization, and this being so, it gives cause to wonder that they did not assimilate even the elements of culture and mechanical knowledge. Is there something in their chromosomes which makes them more backward and different from the people living in the East and West, and if so, we have to ask ourselves, can this inherent disability be bred out?[22]

All the prime ministers of Rhodesia constantly referred to white standards as a measurement of civilization. It never dawned on them that the Africans had their own civilization which they greatly cherished. The rulers of Rhodesia constantly looked down on the Africans as barbarians, as savages, and as inferior to the whites.

So blinkered are the whites of Rhodesia that they have failed to see and to appreciate the richness of African culture.

So arrogant are the whites in Rhodesia that, through the fal-
sification of history they have attempted for years to prove
that the great architectural structure of the Zimbabwe ruins in
central Rhodesia was not built by the Africans. The Zimbabwe ruins, an amazingly huge house of stones built by the
Mashona people centuries before the Europeans ever set foot
in Rhodesia, symbolize how advanced African culture was
long before the white man invaded that part of the world. The
Sinoia Caves, in the northern part of Rhodesia, with their
astonishing tunnels, were built by Africans, again long before
the white man invaded that part of the world. Today these
products of African ingenuity and creativity are tourist attrac-
tions in white Rhodesia. Yet the Africans are said to be primitive and ignorant.

In order to understand the racial prejudice of the whites in
Rhodesia one has to understand their background. The first
seven hundred adventurers who invaded the country in 1890
were a mixture of Englishmen who had failed to acquire
wealth in South Africa and a few Boers who also were in
search of a quick way to wealth. After World War II a number
of Englishmen who had fallen victims of the unemployment of
postwar Britain flocked to Rhodesia. The level of education of
these people was very low, and in general the educational level
of the whites in Rhodesia has remained low. Despite the fact
that it is illegal to keep a child between the ages of six and
fifteen out of school, Rogers and Frantz found in their survey
that 11.2 percent of European children in Rhodesia in 1958
had received less education than required by law. Only 5.8
percent of the whites in Rhodesia had received about seventeen years of education and only 20 percent had received high
school education.[23]

This low educational level has not been boosted by the
immigration policies of the Rhodesian governments. These
governments have encouraged the immigration of whites from
Europe, Canada, and the United States, not on the basis of

skills these immigrants could provide but merely on the basis of the color of their skin. On their arrival in Rhodesia, these new immigrants are provided with good houses and jobs. They earn more than an African university graduate can hope to earn when he leaves the university. The immigrants soon acquire the best houses they have ever had, two cars, and at least two servants per family, which previously they could never have hoped to acquire.

The result of such immigration policies is that the whites who have been attracted to Rhodesia are by and large those who have failed to make it in their native countries. The poorly educated whites who form more than 80 percent of Rhodesian white society cannot compete on equal terms in the labor market. They succeed only because *they are white!* They hate any educated African and strive to humiliate him by insisting that despite his education he is still a "Kaffir."[24]

The white people of Rhodesia have remained very ignorant of the Africans. They are afraid to come into contact with people they regard as inferior. Everything in Rhodesia is segregated. Only at the university and in master-servant relationships do white people come into contact with Africans. Schools, residential areas, transport facilities, and toilet facilities are segregated. Even churches and burial places are segregated. Only the university in Rhodesia is a multiracial institution. The whites agreed to let their students study at the same center with the Africans mainly because Britain made this a precondition for its financial and academic assistance to the university when it was established.

There are scores of white people in Rhodesia who have never spoken a single word to any African except their cooks, garden "boys," and housemaids. Most of the white people in Rhodesia have never spared a moment to listen to any African's opinion. Even the most "liberal" white would recoil if asked, "Would you like your daughter to marry an African?" In fact, in Rhodesia sexual relations between African men and European women are considered an assault on the white man's citadel of privileges. In 1961 Dr. Bernard Chidzero, returning home with a French-Canadian wife and a Ph.D. in political science from McGill University, had his prospective post at the University College of Rhodesia and Nyasaland withdrawn. Patrick Matimba, returning from Europe with a Dutch wife, could not get a residence in any town and was not allowed to reside in any tribal area. Some missionaries provided him and his wife with shelter.

Yet white men have not hesitated to exploit African women. In fact, they were even encouraged to do so by law. In 1903 the white parliament enacted the Immorality and Indecency Act. The act was supposed to protect white women from an imagined capriciousness of the African male while exposing African women to the licentiousness of the white male. The act made it illegal for an African male to have premarital sexual relations with a white woman, but it was not illegal for a white male to have such relations with an African woman. When in 1957 there was an attempt in parliament to amend the law to protect African women from the whims of white men, there was an uproar. Parliament rejected the amendment. By 1964 white men in Rhodesia had fathered and then abandoned about 20,000 children to their African mothers.

This is the Rhodesia in which both the Africans and the whites are trying to make a home, a Rhodesia in which the color of a man's skin is of paramount importance. Patrick Keatley described the situation in Rhodesia very vividly:

> The dilemma facing Britain in Central Africa is the one that has confronted mankind since Cain and Abel: How are we, as brothers, to live together? It is a dilemma that becomes infinitely more exasperating and more acute when one brother is black and the other one white. Why this should be so is a question for the psychiatrist; for the student of politics it is simply a basic and, however unpleasant, inescapable fact.[25]

It is a basic and inescapable fact that the interests of the Africans and the whites in Rhodesia are irreconcilable. The

Africans as well as the whites are struggling for the attainment of their hopes and aspirations. And every day they move nearer to a bloody confrontation, a confrontation that will be fought with racial passion, hatred, and all the worst instincts of mankind. Is there a way to avoid such a racial confrontation? The unpleasant answer is "no." All attempts to avert the crisis must take into account the emotional issue of race and all the prejudices and realities that surround the issue. Rhodesia is past the point where the issue could be amicably settled. Racism flows in the blood of the whites of Rhodesia, and the Africans have finally concluded that the whites and their system must go before Africans can reclaim their lost dignity.

Economic Factors

Before 1965 Rhodesia's economy showed impressive growth for a developing country. In 1947 foreign investment was about $39 million; in 1949 it had doubled, and in 1951 it was $150 million. The net domestic product at current prices rose from $81 million in 1939 to $753 million in 1961; fixed capital formation between 1946 and 1961 amounted on the average to $150 million.[26] Looking at Salisbury, the capital city, Professor Thomas Franck observed, "Salisbury in transition looks like a double exposure of midtown Manhattan and Dead Man's Gulch."[27]

This economic growth was achieved at the expense of 96 percent of the population and is enjoyed by the 4 percent who by accident of birth are white. The African has been left with less than minimum resources for survival.

To the African, land holds a deep meaning that transcends the needs of his day-to-day livelihood. On land is based the African's traditional social system, his security as an individual and as a member of a family, his ties with his ancestors and therefore the basis of his religion. Take away the land and African society ceases to exist; the security of the individual and the family is threatened.

Land holds a dear meaning to Rhodesian whites as well. It means the acquisition of wealth, the attraction of white immigrants, and subsequently the consolidation of political power in white hands. To both the Africans and the whites, land means survival and the good things of life. From the early days of his appearance in Zimbabwe, the white man wanted to reserve the best lands for his own utilization and settlement. Those parts of the country having better soil and rainfall and well served with road and rail communications were to be reserved for the white man. Unmindful of the needs of the Africans, the white man removed most of them by force from their traditional fertile lands, driving them to settle in the hot, unproductive, and at times unhealthy parts of the country. Under the provisions of the 1969 Land Tenure Act, today's whites (numbering 250,000) enjoy 50 percent of the land while the five million Africans have the other 50 percent.

The bulk of white-owned land is divided into large estates. According to the government farming statistics for 1962, less than 2 percent of the European farm land was allotted to farms of less than 1,000 acres each, and over 33 percent of the European land was held in farms of over 20,000 acres each. The report reveals that, in 1962, 3,840,000 acres of European land were "farms on which no agricultural activities were carried on."[28] Although this land is idle, it is considered politically expedient that it be denied to the Africans.

African lands are located in sandy areas. According to Kenneth Brown, a British agricultural specialist who worked for six years for the Rhodesian government:

> Most of the native area is poor soil, usually granite sand known as class III. In many parts of the country it is quite embarrassing to drive through an European area into a native area. Change in soil type coincides almost exactly with the boundary line and is startlingly obvious: An example is the Salisbury and Shamva road.[29]

The successive Rhodesian governments have not been embarrassed by such situations. As far back as 1958 a Rhodesian government report noted that "with a rapidly increasing native population, the land problem becomes more acute each successive year."[30] This report conceded that there were more than 337,000 African families entitled to land rights who had not been given a square inch of the land. Despite this report, it did not occur to the Rhodesian government that African lands should be increased. In fact, subsequent government reports acknowledge that between 1950 and 1960 about 110,000 African families were removed from their homes just to make room for more unused reserved lands for whites. Bulldozers demolished homes and villages in which African families lived, destroyed crops by which they supported themselves, and desecrated their ancestral burial places. This was done to create lands for whites who had not yet been born or had not yet arrived in Rhodesia.

Besides depriving the Africans of their land, the Rhodesian government has limited the number of cattle the African can own. Unmindful of the fact that cattle have been regarded by Africans as the symbol of wealth, dowry for marriage, and source of food, the Rhodesian Legislature passed in 1951 the Native Land Husbandry Act. This Act provided that each family should own only six acres of agricultural lands and only eight head of cattle—four oxen for ploughing, two calves and two cows. Africans were forced to sell or slaughter many of their cattle. In fact, government officials roamed about the country selecting the cattle the Africans had to sell to the white people. Generally the best were chosen for such sales.

Under such a system, the economic position of the African has deteriorated while that of the whites has improved tremendously. The whites in Rhodesia have tended to give themselves credit for the economic development of Rhodesia before 1965. They have tended to look at this development as the result of the "ingeniousness" which they believe is the monopoly of whites. They very conveniently forget that the African has immensely contributed to the economy of Rhodesia. In European agriculture alone, in 1965, 273,800 Africans labored day and night to produce the tobacco and sugar the white man prizes. Some 43,600 Africans worked in mining and 71,000 Africans worked in manufacturing.[31] And yet this contribution of the African to the economy has not been recognized either through wage remuneration or through the improvement of his living conditions.

In 1961 Africans who worked in white man's agriculture were paid $6 a month per head while a white employee was paid $183 a month. An African miner was paid $10 a month while a white miner was paid $318. In the manufacturing industry an African employee earned $20 a month while a white employee received $300. On the average in 1961 the African wage in Rhodesia was $190.60 a year while that of the white man was $2,894.[32]

Unemployment for the African is rampant in Rhodesia. According to official statistics, of the 48,000 African sixteen-year-olds who leave school every year, none since 1965 has been able to get a job, and before 1962 less than one-twentieth were absorbed into the money economy. The despoiling of land from the Africans has made thousands of them flock to towns in search of some means of livelihood. The Native Husbandry Act alone deprived more than 128,000 African families of their lands to make more room for whites. In 1962, 80,000 Africans who had been previously employed in the money economy were out on the streets looking for work. Unemployed Africans are invited to work on white men's farms, their remuneration being corn meal and beans.

When the Africans showed reluctance to working on white farms, Parliament passed the Vagrancy Act, whose Section 2 (B) describes a vagrant as "any person wandering about and unable to show that he has employment or visible and sufficient means of subsistence." Section 4 (1) (A) and (B) provides a penalty for any person who "harbors any vagrant, or suffers or permits any vagrant to reside on land or premises owned or occupied by such person." This means that a father cannot allow his son who has not been admitted to school because of the education restrictions and who fails to find work to reside on his small piece of land. Using this law the Rhodesian governments have mobilized unemployed Africans for the purpose of providing white farmers with cheap labor. Those Africans who have been lucky enough to be employed in towns live in deplorable, subhuman conditions. Eighty percent of the accommodations provided for the Africans near towns are for single men who usually live four to a room. Thus an African working in the money economy is not able to stay with his family. If an African succeeds in securing a house in one of the African townships he cannot allow a visitor to spend a night in his home without the permission of the white superintendent. Houses in the townships are often raided in search of "illegal" visitors. Privacy is violated, mothers insulted in the presence of their sons, and fathers belittled before their children. If a man loses his job he automatically loses his house in the township, and yet he cannot go to his traditional home because he has no land there; at any time a jobless African can be picked up as a vagrant.

The white man can have as many houses as he wants. He can have as many white visitors as he wants and they can spend as many days and nights in his home as he wants. A white man who chooses not to work is not described as a vagrant and does not lose his house.

In Rhodesia the white man enjoys the good life that African labor and resources provide. To expect the white man willingly to share this good life with the African is to expect too much from human nature. He has a privileged position in Rhodesia; he will hold fast to it and resist all the forces that work to deprive him of what he considers to be exclusively his. And yet the African cannot be expected to anguish eternally at the feet of the white man. He has seen the resources of his motherland exploited for the benefit of a small alien community. He has seen his labor exploited and never rewarded. The harder he works for the white man in Rhodesia, the more insults he gets from the beneficiary of his labor.

The African, just as the white man, wants to enjoy the good

life, to build a home for his posterity, and to die in peace.
These things have been denied to him by the white man. He
has no recourse except to wrestle them from the white man,
who of course will resist, with a bloody confrontation ensu-
ing. Rhodesia is a wealthy country whose economic resources
could enable all its inhabitants to live as happily as humanly
possible. But the greed of the white man, the desire to pile
wealth upon wealth in complete disregard of those who
hunger, of those who contribute to the wealth by their sweat,
has intensified the hatred patterned to the color of a person's
skin. The end of this greed will come only after tragic events;
it is too late for white and black to live in harmony in
Rhodesia.

Educational Factors

While attempting to raise the educational standards of white
people in Rhodesia, the Rhodesian governments have been
very reluctant to provide any education for the African except
for the purpose of providing good servants for the white man.
Those Africans who stubbornly seek more and better education soon find themselves, after achieving their cherished goal,
joining the unemployment lines.

Most of the African education, as will be seen in Chapter 4,
is in the hands of the churches. The government has claimed
that it subsidizes African schools. But an examination of the
facts belies this claim. The Commonwealth Fact Sheets reveal
shocking statistics. Taking the period before the Rhodesian
Front came to power in 1962, since it is said that in this period
the African made "remarkable" advances in education under
what were thought to be "progressive" governments, one
notes the following: In 1948 the Rhodesian government provided seven primary schools for the Africans; by 1953 the
number had been increased to sixteen, and by 1960 there were
fifty government-supported African primary schools in the
whole country. On the secondary school level, in 1948 there

was one government-supported African school, and by 1953 there had been *no* increase. By 1960 the number had been increased to only five. These figures must be read together with those of the African school-age population. In 1960 the African population was 3.5 million, half of which was below the age of seventeen and thus mostly of school-age. And yet the Rhodesian government provided only fifty primary schools, only five secondary schools, and only four technical and vocational schools for the African. In 1969 the Rhodesian government spent about $300 per white child in school per year, while it provided only $28 per African child in school per year.

In 1961 nearly half of the African pupils left school after two years. According to a survey conducted by J. Rogaly for the *London Economist*, five years of education "is the best that most African school children could expect. This means learning to read and write in African languages; very simple English reading and writing; elementary arithmetic; nature study; and local history and geography."[33] Of the 15,424 African children who were lucky enough in 1961 to have eight years of education, only 2,539 were admitted to the first year of secondary-school education, and only 364 completed four years of secondary-school education.[34] These figures include students in both missionary and government schools.

Despite this tight control of African education, the white people of Rhodesia feel insecure, especially since more and more Africans have begun receiving education outside Rhodesia. This insecurity has driven them to seek refuge in their color, and therefore has intensified the racism that characterizes Rhodesia.

Political Factors

The distribution of power and the use of it is the major problem in Rhodesia. As we shall see in Chapter 2, from the very beginning the white man did not intend to share political power with the Africans. Rhodesia was to be made "safe for the permanent survival of Western European Civilization." Today voting power is still not shared with the Africans. Under the provisions of the 1969 Constitution, Rhodesia's powerless Senate has ten members elected by whites, ten elected by Africans, and three appointed by the government, thus guaranteeing a white majority every time. Representation in Rhodesia's chief governing body, the House of Assembly, consists of fifty European members and sixteen African members (of whom only eight are directly elected, the others being elected by electoral colleges of chiefs, headmen, and councilors).[35] Africans comprise 96 percent of the population but are directly represented by only 12 percent of the House. The inequity is staggering.

The constitution provides that more African seats will be added to the House after Africans contribute at least 24 percent of the national income tax, but there is never to be more than parity in the House (i.e., never more than half white seats and half black).

The 1969 Constitution was the central issue in the 1971 Home-Smith Agreement, which was Britain's attempt at settling with her rebel colony and assuring eventual majority rule there. But even this Agreement, which was eventually rejected by the Africans, did not guarantee equal representation in Rhodesia for the foreseeable future. Instead, it sought to forestall majority rule for generations to come.

Like the 1969 Constitution, the Home-Smith Agreement provided two types of qualifications for voters: the higher voters' roll and the lower voters' roll. Table 1 shows the qualifications for each roll.

Since the qualifications for the higher roll would have been difficult for Africans to meet, this roll would have been almost exclusively European, while the lower roll would have been predominantly African. As long as the government controlled the salaries and education available to the Africans, this distribution would remain the same.

TABLE I
VOTING QUALIFICATIONS IN RHODESIA
UNDER PROPOSED HOME-SMITH AGREEMENT[36]

QUALIFICATIONS FOR HIGHER VOTERS ROLL:	QUALIFICATIONS FOR LOWER VOTERS ROLL:
1 annual income of $1200 or ownership of $3600 of immovable property **or**	**1** annual income of $600 or ownership of $1100 of immovable property
2 annual income of $1200 or ownership of $2400 of immovable property and 4 years' secondary education of prescribed standard	**or** **2** annual income of $300 or ownership of $600 of immovable property and 2 years' secondary education of prescribed standard
	or
	3 annual income of $430 or ownership of $800 of immovable property and voter must be at least 30 years old
	or
	4 annual income of $300 or ownership of $600 of immovable property and voter at least 30 years old and have completed course of primary education
	or
	5 voter is a kraal (village) head with following of 20 or more heads of families.

The Home-Smith Agreement further provided that

additional African seats will be created (by two) when the number of voters registered on the African higher roll equals 6 percent of the number of voters then registered on the European roll; when the number of voters registered on the African higher roll equals 12 percent of the number of voters then registered on the European roll, a further two additional African seats will become due; further additional African seats will become due, two at a time, for each proportionate increase of 6 percent in the number of voters registered on the African higher roll, until thirty-four additional African seats have been created, thus resulting in parity in the numbers of African and European members in the House of Assembly.[37]

However, since the voting rolls would be determined by income and educational qualifications, the regime could control the speed by which Africans obtain additional seats in the House of Assembly. And even if the regime allowed African income and educational growth to continue at the current rate, the attainment of African majority rule through the Home-Smith mechanism would still be beyond the sight not only of the present generation but of three to five more generations to come. Smith himself said on BBC Television that he did not know "what the situation would be in 100 or 1000 years." And he added, "I won't be here, will I?"[38]

As if to hoodwink the Africans, the British government agreed to provide $12 million a year for ten years to improve the African educational and economic situation. But the provision was not without controls. Part of Section VI of the Agreement reads as follows: "The British Government will provide up to 5 million pounds per year for a period of ten years in capital aid and technical assistance to be applied to purposes and projects to be agreed with the Rhodesian Government . . . . "[39]

It was the Rhodesian regime that would have determined which projects would be financed. The Africans rejected this Anglo-Rhodesian proposed settlement and, for now, Britain for the first time has respected the wishes of the Africans by not putting the settlement proposals into effect.

It seems unlikely that the whites in Rhodesia will want to give Africans their rightful share in the political process, for the franchise has remained one of the most prized instruments of political power in the hands of white Rhodesians. As we will see in the following chapters, each time there has been a small increase in the total number of Africans who qualify for the vote, the whites of Rhodesia have revised the qualifications, raising the income, property, and educational requirements. The whites enjoy political power in Rhodesia and should not be expected to give it up. It was the English statesman, Edmund Burke, who said, "Those who have been once intoxicated with power, even though but for one year, can never willingly abandon it."

Since the Africans can never hope to achieve political power by the vote, they must search for other means to attain it. Without the attainment of political power they will continue to be subjected to insults and humiliation in the land of their birth; they will continue to suffer deprivations. Life as the Africans know it will continue to be disrupted and they will continue to witness unfulfilled dreams. It is only a matter of time before the white man is pitted against the black man. The white man will fight to defend what he claims as his own, and the black man will fight to reclaim what is rightfully his own. The confrontation will be bloody.

NOTES

1. See Stanlake Samkange, *Origins of Rhodesia* (New York: Frederick A. Praeger, 1968), p. 2. See also A.J. Wills, *Introduction to the History of Central Africa* (London: Oxford University Press, 1967), p. 12.

2. Samkange, *Origins*. Cf. map, p. 171.

3. *Ibid.*, p. 4.

4. *Ibid.*, p. 58.

5. *Ibid.*, p. 72.

6. *Ibid.*, pp. 73–74.

7. *Ibid.*, pp. 78–79.

8. *Ibid.*, p. 87.

9. T.O. Ranger, *Revolt in Southern Rhodesia 1896–1897* (Evanston: Northwestern University Press, 1967), p. 46.

10. *Ibid.*, p. 127.

11. *Ibid.*, p. 192.

12. Nora S. Kane, *The World's View: The Story of Southern Rhodesia* (London: Cassell, 1954), p. 104.

13. Samkange, *Origins*, pp. 240–57.

14. Samkange quotes these words from official documents. See *ibid.*, p. 241.

15. *Ibid.*, p. 242.

16. *Ibid.*, p. 240.

17. African National Council Manifesto, March 10, 1972.

18. Patrick Keatley, *The Politics of Partnership* (London: Penguin Books, 1963), p. 23.

19. Kane, *World's View*, p. 169.

20. Keatley, *Politics*, p. 75.

21. *Ibid.*, p. 291.

22. Colin Leys, *European Politics in Southern Rhodesia* (Oxford University Press, 1959), p. 259.

23. C. Rogers and C. Frantz, *Racial Themes in Southern Rhodesia* (New Haven: Yale University Press, 1962), p. 66.

24. "Kaffir" means an unbeliever. It has come to mean an inferior person. In Rhodesia it is used for an African.

25. Keatley, *Politics*, p. 9.

26. Giovanni Arrighi, "Rhodesia: Class and Power," *New Left Review*, no. 39, September-October 1966, p. 45.

27. Thomas M. Franck, *Race and Nationalism: The Struggle for Power in Rhodesia-Nyasaland* (New York: Fordham University Press, 1960), p. 273.

28. *Report on the Agricultural Production of Southern Rhodesia, Northern Rhodesia and Nyasaland 1962*, Salisbury, 1963.

29. Kenneth Brown, *Land in Southern Rhodesia* (Salisbury, n.d.).

30. *Annual Report of the Chief Native Commissioner*, Salisbury, 1958.

31. *National Accounts and Balance of Payments of Rhodesia 1968*, Salisbury, 1969.

32. *Federal Census of Population and Employees*, Salisbury, 1962, pp. 4 and 14.

33. See Document W. P. No. 4163 submitted to the U.N. Security Council, August 1963, p. 61.

34. *Southern Rhodesia Annual Report of the Director of Native Education*, Salisbury, 1961, Table II.

35. *Rhodesia, Proposals for a Settlement, 1971*, London, CMND 4835, p. 8.

36. *Ibid.*, p. 18.

37. *Ibid.*, p. 12.

38. See *Washington Post*, December 2, 1971.

39. *Proposals for a Settlement*, 1971, p. 16.

CHAPTER 2

Paternalism as "Liberalism"

From 1923 until the Rhodesian Front came to power in December 1962, the Rhodesian governments were considered by Britain and later by the Western world as progressive liberal governments. And yet during these forty years these governments put Africans in chains and continued to tighten the chains year after year. Most laws that the present Rhodesian government uses to incarcerate the African were enacted before the Rhodesian Front came to power. The Rhodesian Front government does today what its predecessors did before it; today the action is called "reactionary" and "oppressive," while before the RF government such action was called "liberal." Until December 1962 the Rhodesian governments adopted a paternalistic approach in their dealings with the Africans. And many people mistake paternalism for liberalism.

In the affairs of state, paternalism is always the product of a superiority-inferiority relationship between people. Those who consider themselves superior adopt a paternalistic attitude toward those they consider inferior. In nearly all cases those who are the "beneficiaries" of this paternalism tend to resent such an attitude, since to accept the paternalism of those who regard themselves as superior is to agree that the "beneficiaries" of the paternalism are inferior. Thus paternalism becomes an instrument of oppression and not a hallmark of liberalism.

Politics Before 1923

White paternalism in Rhodesia began with white settlement itself. One of the clearest indications of this was the exclusion of Africans from the political scene by the whites. From earliest times and with the active encouragement of Britain the whites regarded the African as something outside the political system of the country, incapable of comprehending the mechanics of politics. Although the white man has since 1890 wielded political power in Rhodesia, he has been painfully conscious that he is in the minority in the country and that if no controls are inserted into the political system power could easily move into the hands of the Africans. In 1903 the white people even complained that the little education that was made available to the African was a threat to their control of the country. *The Rhodesia Herald* declared, "The black peril will become a reality when the results of our misguided system of education have taken root and when a veneer of European civilization struggles with the innate savage nature."[1] The possibility of political power in the hands of such "savages" was to be prevented. Since the white man controlled the educational and economic benefits available to the African, a qualitative franchise based on educational, financial, and property qualifications became the white man's strongest mechanism to exclude the African from the political system.

The first Franchise Law was established through the Southern Rhodesian Order in Council Proclamation Number 17, issued in 1898. According to this proclamation, the vote was given to people with the following qualifications: (1) British male subjects, except lunatics and convicts, who were (2) over the age of twenty-one, (3) literate enough to file and read electoral application forms, and (4) earning a bona

fide income of at least fifty pounds a year or owning immovable property worth seventy-five pounds. Under these qualifications every adult white man in Rhodesia qualified to be a
voter—while no African in 1898 could meet the fourth qualification. By 1912 only about a dozen Africans could qualify to
vote, and indeed they did register. But the very fact that a
dozen Africans had qualified seemed an ominous development
to the white men of Rhodesia. They began to search for ways
to halt this "threat." In 1917 they raised the income qualifications to 100 pounds a year and the value of the immovable
property to 150 pounds.

With complete disregard for the African, Britain decided in
1922 to hold a referendum in Rhodesia to enable the white
people to choose between amalgamating with South Africa or
attaining self-government status under some form of British
supervision. In holding this referendum Britain did not even
consider that the African existed and ought to be consulted.
The African was only an unwanted nuisance. The white people chose the road toward self-governing status. According to
Mrs. E. Tawse-Jolie, one of the early settlers, by choosing the
self-governing status every white man in Rhodesia became
"intolerably Rhodesian." She goes on to note that had the
white settlers ever suspected that one day they would be asked
to share power with the Africans, they definitely would have
voted to join South Africa.[2]

In 1923 Britain granted Rhodesia a constitution that made it
autonomous in its internal affairs. The Legislative Assembly
with thirty seats was filled completely with whites. No provision was made for African representation. Thus one step more
was taken, with British connivance, towards the consolidation
of white supremacy in Rhodesia.

"Protective" Legislation

Britain supported the superiority-inferiority relationship
between the white immigrants and the Africans and adopted a

"protective" attitude towards the African. In the 1923 Constitution, Britain inscribed Section 28 (a), which read in part that "any law, save in respect of the supply of arms, ammunition or liquor to natives, whereby natives may be subjected or made liable to any conditions, disabilities, or restrictions to which persons of European descent are not subjected or made liable . . . " had to be approved by the British government through the governor. Section 31 of the Constitution further provided that the British Crown could, on the advice of the British government, disallow any Rhodesian law within one year of its enactment if such a law were discriminatory against the Africans. The idea was to protect the "inferior" Africans from the whims of the "superior" white men.

Let us examine how these sections of the Constitution were upheld. We will begin with matters of little consequence. It was assumed that if the Africans were allowed to drink European beer and liquors they would go wild. After all, Britain and the whites of Rhodesia believed the Africans possessed some "innate savage" characteristics. Britain was unmindful of the fact that many Africans drank Kachasu, a gin that is by far stronger than any liquor the white man has ever marketed. However, it was not until 1961 that the Africans were legally allowed to drink European liquors.

In 1925 Britain appointed the Morris Carter Commission to recommend how the land of Rhodesia should be divided between the whites and the Africans. Giving evidence before this commission, N.H. Wilson, a senior official of the Native Affairs Department, said, "We are in this country because we represent a higher civilization, because we are better men. It is our only excuse for having taken the land."[3] Wilson warned that the commission, in dividing the land, should not create "poor whites." "To allow this to come to pass," he said, "would be a calamity to the state, a cruel injustice to our own race and children, and a gross betrayal to the civilization in which we may be supposed to believe."[4]

The Carter Report, which catered to the fears of the whites, became the basis of the Land Apportionment Act of 1930. This Act divided the land according to race and became what the whites claimed was the "Magna Carta" of the white people in Rhodesia—and the source of intense bitterness for the Africans. The Act maintained the same division of land regardless of changes in population levels until it was strengthened in 1971 by the Land Tenure Act. The Land Apportionment Act apportioned 41 million acres of the best lands to the whites, who were never more than 5 percent of the total population. The Africans, who comprise at least 95 percent, were apportioned 44 million acres. The Land Tenure Act was later to increase the land apportioned to whites and divide the land into two exactly equal parts.

Although the Land Apportionment Act was discriminatory, Britain did not invoke Sections 28 and 31 of the constitution: it was argued that the Act was in the interest of the Africans. It was said that if the government did not designate certain areas for the Africans, the white men would go about dispossessing the Africans of their land. The fact that 95 percent of the population was alloted 44 million acres of land, while 5 percent of the population was alloted 41 million acres was not considered unfair and unjust. The fact that the land for the Africans was infertile and that for the whites was rich was of little significance to the British.

The Land Husbandry Act, passed in 1951, made it illegal for Africans to own more than six acres of land and eight head of cattle per family. Again Britain did not invoke Sections 28 and 31 of the Constitution; again it was argued that the Act was in the interest of the Africans. The Act was meant to "protect" African land from soil erosion and overcrowding. The African was being "protected" by being thrown off his own land and by being deprived of his own means of livelihood without being given any alternatives.

There are numerous laws in Rhodesian statute books which are discriminatory to the Africans. They were enacted under the 1923 Constitution. And yet Britain never raised a finger.

Not only the Land Apportionment Act and the Land Husbandry Act but also the Vagrants Act (directed against Africans without jobs or land to return to), the African Registration and Identification Act (requiring Africans to carry passes), the African Affairs Act (a general act to control Africans), and many others have dehumanized the Africans of Rhodesia. Every one of them was described as "protecting" the interests of the African.

"Liberals" and Conservatives

Actually, liberalism in any form has always been rejected in Rhodesia by the majority of the whites and the majority of the Africans. In 1932 the governing party, the Rhodesia Party, was divided into two wings, the conservatives and those who considered themselves "liberal." In fact the latter group was not liberal by any definition; it was only less conservative than the former group. The point of dispute between the two factions of the party was how far to enforce the strict territorial segregation of the races as provided in the Land Apportionment Act. The conservatives wanted a complete separation of the races; the less conservative group wanted the separation of the races to be mitigated by considerations of white requirements of African labor. The conservatives split from the Rhodesia Party and formed the Reform Party. In the elections of 1933 the Reform Party, led by Godfrey Huggins, was elected to power. Thus the white electorate rejected the least sign of white liberalism.

But by 1942 the conservatives of 1932 had become lesser conservatives on the Rhodesian political spectrum. The issue in dispute was how far the African was to be educated. Godfrey Huggins wanted the African to be given a little more education, but the conservatives of 1942 led by J.H. Smith wanted the African to be given only such education as would make him a disciplined industrial laborer or servant. Smith and his conservatives formed their own party, which they ironically called the Liberal Party. By 1945 Godfrey Huggins had changed the name of his party to the United Party and merged it with the Rhodesian Party (from which he had split). His United Party controlled twenty-four out of thirty seats in the Legislative Assembly. But in the elections of 1946 he lost twelve seats to the conservative Liberal Party and remained in power only by forming a coalition with the five Labor Party members. The electorate of Rhodesia indicated very strong support for extreme conservatism; the less conservative party had to scratch for support to get a working majority in the Rhodesian Parliament.

By 1958 the less conservative United Party, which was the governing party, had changed its name to the United Federal Party (UFP), and the conservatives had banded together in the Dominion Party (DP). When Garfield Todd, leader of the UFP and Prime Minister of Rhodesia, attempted to appease the Africans by improving the living conditions of the educated few, there was an uproar in his party. He was sacked and replaced by Sir Edgar Whitehead. The more conservative faction of the UFP was in control, although this faction was still less conservative than the Dominion Party.

Todd has been called a "liberal" interested in African advancement mainly because of what he said about the Africans and not because of what he actually did to enhance African interests. Todd is accurately portrayed by his fellow "liberal", Theodore Bull, in *Crisis of Color: Rhodesia*. This is what Bull says about the downfall of Todd in 1958 as the Prime Minister of Rhodesia:

> It is crucial to remember that Todd was removed, not because of what he did, but because of what he said. While in office he was not an activist for widely increased African rights by any stretch of the imagination; the simple threat, or belief that he might become so, led to his downfall.[5]

The "Liberal" Response
to African Strikes and Demonstrations

Although Africans were hardly included in Rhodesian politics, they did make their voices heard through several attempts.

at passive resistance. The government's response, even when under the control of a "liberal" party, was always harsh. For example, when in 1948 B.B. Burombo and his African Voice Association called for a general strike of Africans, the government of Sir Godfrey Huggins did not hesitate to use brute force to break the strike.[6] In fact, as a result of the strike efforts of the Africans in 1948, the Huggins Government passed the Subversive Activities Act of 1950 through the Rhodesian Parliament. This act gave the police the right to use firearms to disperse people. It was also because of the fears generated among the Europeans by the strikes of 1948 that Burombo's African Voice Association was temporarily banned in May 1951. The government of Rhodesia wanted to be certain that this organization would not again attempt to organize Africans into strikes.

The following administration did not react any differently to African strikes. When in 1956 the African workers at the Wankie mines went on strike, Todd, who today is proclaimed by the white world as the greatest European liberal in Rhodesia, decided to request the troops of the Federation of Rhodesia and Nyasaland to suppress the strike by force. Todd did not investigate whether the striking Africans had genuine labor grievances that needed to be attended to.

The government response was the same in regard to demonstrations to "coerce" the government. For example, the Beadle Tribunal was appointed in 1959 under the Preventive Detention Act to pass judgment on whether the African political organization known as the African National Congress had violated the laws of Rhodesia. The Beadle Tribunal, under the chairmanship of the present Chief Justice of Rhodesia, Sir Hugh Beadle, found the ANC guilty of (1) exciting disobedience and hostility to the laws and lawful authorities of the country; (2) exciting racial hostility and disseminating subversive propaganda; (3) coercing the government by demonstrations, processions, and strikes; and (4) misinterpreting and falsifying facts with a view to bringing the government and Europeans into disrepute.

"Liberal" Prime Minister Whitehead, who succeeded Todd, also believed in using what he termed "the iron rod" against the Africans. In July 1960 Michael Mawema, then the leader of the National Democratic Party (NDP)—an African political organization which attempted to mobilize Africans under the slogan of "Majority Rule Now"—was arrested. The Africans in Harare Township decided to march towards the center of Salisbury. They were unarmed and were protesting peacefully against the arrest of their leader. Sir Edgar Whitehead reacted by sending armed police to break up the demonstration. The police showered a volley of bullets on the unarmed demonstrators, killing some and wounding many. The Rhodesian government reported that twelve demonstrators had been killed, but the NDP counted thirty-six.[7]

The Whitehead government attempted to explain the use of police firearms on unarmed demonstrators by saying that the Africans were rioting, burning, and looting stores. It is true that the Africans rioted and burned down buildings. But what is very often overlooked is the sequence of events of that fateful July. Let the record be corrected. The police raided and ransacked the offices of the NDP on July 7, 1960. On July 19 they raided the homes of NDP officials and arrested Michael Mawema and Leopold Takawira, leading officials of the party. On July 20, 25,000 unarmed Africans began their march towards the center of Salisbury, demanding to see Prime Minister Whitehead. The police fired on the demonstrators, and casualties resulted. Only then did the Africans, angry over the cold-blooded murder of their brothers and sisters, begin to stone police cars. African school-children joined their elders the next day and the demonstration turned into rioting. The police responded with more bullets, increasing the number of dead and wounded.[8]

In July 1961 the Africans went on a general strike protest

because the 1961 Constitution, which they had rejected, was being put before a predominantly white electorate in a referendum. Whitehead deployed 24,000 troops, armed with Sten guns and self-loading rifles, in the African townships and used brute force to break the African strike efforts.[9]

The governments of Rhodesia, including those led by men of "liberal" persuasion, demonstrated that they did not tolerate strikes or demonstrations by the Africans. These were considered "lawlessness." And Sir Edgar Whitehead promised that "lawlessness will be put down with a rod of iron."[10]

The "Liberal" Tredgold Commission

By 1949 a number of associations, clubs, and parties had come together to form the White Rhodesian Council, pledged to the survival of white supremacy in Rhodesia. The Council declared in 1951:

> As the natives are so far behind, it is imperative that there shall be white supremacy for hundreds of years . . . Actually it is not their country, in fact it is less so than that of Europeans from the point of view of being a conquered territory.[11]

The Council attracted many leading white businessmen, farmers, and politicians. Winston Field, Prime Minister from 1962 to 1964, was a member of the Council. This organization symbolized both the fears of the whites and their efforts to make Rhodesia safe for the white man.

By 1951 the whites were fearful of an African takeover of Rhodesia. As they watched the growing registration of Africans as voters they felt threatened. In 1939 this feared "growth" was only seventy Africans on the roll out of a total of 28,296 voters. In 1951 the whites demanded the revision of the electoral laws. Parliament enacted the 1951 Electoral Law providing that a voter had to earn a bona fide income of not less than 240 pounds or own an immovable property worth at least 500 pounds. Five years later 560 Africans out of an African population of almost two and a half million qualified as voters. The whites at this time numbered 177,124, of whom more than half were of voting age, and all of the latter qualified to vote because they met the income requirement. Nevertheless, they panicked at this "quick rise" in the number of African voters. The government appointed the Tredgold Commission to review the franchise.

Robert Tredgold was the Chief Justice of the Federation of Rhodesia and Nyasaland and was considered one of the most liberal whites in Rhodesia. But in 1956 Tredgold and his commission did not forget their task: the maintenance of white supremacy in Rhodesia. The Tredgold Commission Report recommended ways to safeguard white political power in Rhodesia. Paragraph 590 (e) of the report reads as follows:

> The European section of the electorate should feel itself adequately protected against the possibility that it might be politically overwhelmed by the backward and illiterate sections of the African population, susceptible to unnecessary appeals to African Nationalism.[12]

Such was the conclusion of the most "liberal" commission that ever sat in Rhodesia. The Commission recommended that there should be two types of qualifications for voters: the special roll and the ordinary roll. Those Rhodesian citizens with a bona fide income of 180 pounds a year were to be registered in the special roll. Since all Europeans earned far more than 180 pounds a year in 1956, the special roll was to be for the Africans. The ordinary roll was primarily meant for Europeans because its qualifications were such that few Africans could meet them: (1) income of 720 pounds a year or immovable property worth 1,500 pounds plus literacy in English, or (2) income of 480 pounds a year or immovable property of 1,000 pounds plus Standard VI (grade eight) education, or (3) income of 300 pounds a year or immovable property of 500 pounds plus Form IV (grade twelve) education. No African with bare literacy in English could ever hope to earn 720 pounds a year. But most Europeans could meet this first qualification. No African in Rhodesia with only eight years of education could ever hope to earn 480 pounds a year. In these qualifications for franchise the further one went in school the less income was needed for one to register as a voter. And yet the longer one's education the higher one's income was apt to be. Thus most Europeans qualified to be voters since their white skins guaranteed them a high annual income no matter how low their education was. But only the African college graduates and those few Africans on whom fortune had smiled could register as ordinary voters. In 1956 Rhodesia had only a handful of such Africans.

The Tredgold Commission, realizing that some European wives do not work and therefore could not qualify as ordinary voters, and fearful of the remote possibility that there might be some Europeans who could not meet the income qualifications, recommended in Paragraph 735 (iii) that the income of husband and wife should be added together and the total income should be deemed to be the income of each. This recommendation sought to make nearly every adult white person in Rhodesia a voter on the ordinary roll. The Commission knew that in most cases African wives do not earn a salary, and in those cases in which both the husband and the wife worked their joint income would not come near to qualifying them as voters on the ordinary roll.

The Tredgold Commission was afraid that Africans, by enrolling under the special qualifications, could in time overwhelm the Europeans registered under the ordinary qualifications. It proposed that in any election the votes of people registered on the special roll should never count as more than one-half the votes cast by voters registered on the ordinary roll in the same constituency. For example, in a constituency of 600 ordinary voters and 200 special voters, each vote would count as one because the total number of special votes would not be more than one-half of the ordinary votes cast. But should 500 ordinary voters and 300 special voters cast ballots, the special votes of every election candidate would be reduced so that only a total of 250 special votes would be counted. Suppose that in a three-cornered election

Candidate A obtained 130 special votes
Candidate B obtained 110 special votes
Candidate C obtained 60 special votes

After the votes had been reduced

Candidate A would get $\frac{130}{300} \times \frac{250}{1} = 108$ 1/3 votes

Candidate B would get $\frac{110}{300} \times \frac{250}{1} = 91$ 2/3 votes

Candidate C would get $\frac{60}{300} \times \frac{250}{1} = 50$ votes

The idea in this system was to appear to be enfranchising the African and yet to neutralize his vote in the counting procedures. Let it be remembered that this Commission was considered the most liberal commission that ever sat in Rhodesia. The Commission was well aware of the fears the Europeans had about enfranchising the Africans. In fact, when the Tredgold Commission Report was presented to the Rhodesian Parliament both government members and opposition members of Parliament joined hands in protesting against the "liberalness" of the special voters' qualifications. Parliament raised the special voters' qualifications from the recommended income requirements of 180 pounds to 204 pounds plus an adequate knowledge of English, or 120 pounds plus an educational qualification of Form II (grade ten). Parliament also specified that qualifications were to be reviewed every three years and enrollment of special voters was to be closed whenever special voters numbered 20 percent of the ordinary voters.[13]

The Tredgold Commission demonstrated that liberalism meant *appearing* to distribute political power evenly. Even the

most "liberal" whites did not intend to actually give Africans
equal voting privileges. The idea was always to "protect" the
African from responsibilities that he was supposedly unable to
handle.

"Partnership" of the Races

Paternalism in Rhodesia in particular and in Central Africa
in general reached its peak in the years between 1952 and
1962. In 1953 Southern Rhodesia, Northern Rhodesia (Zambia), and Nyasaland (Malawi) were joined into the Federation
of Rhodesia and Nyasaland. The Africans in the three territories were strenuously and vehemently opposed to this
Federation on the grounds that it was in furtherance of white
supremacy in Central Africa.[14] Britain and the whites in Central Africa argued that the Federation was an experiment in
partnership of races, in multiracialism.[15] But the whites in
Central Africa were never in doubt that the partnership they
were seeking in the Federation was the partnership—as expressed by Sir Godfrey Huggins, the first Prime Minister of
the Federation—of "a horse and a rider." It was stressed, even
in official circles, that partners are not necessarily equal.
There is always a senior partner and a junior partner. The
African was the junior partner, the horse, and the white man
was the senior partner, the rider.

Nowhere was the unequalness of the partners more clearly
expressed than in the distribution of political power in the
Federation of Rhodesia and Nyasaland. One year before the
Federation was dissolved there were about 8,500,000 people
in the three territories.[16] Of these only about 300,000 were
white. The Africans outnumbered the whites by a ratio of
26:1. But of the 91,767 people on the federal voters' roll only
1,164 were Africans. In other words the white voters outnumbered the African voters by a ratio of 79:1.[17] Of the
fifty-nine seats in the Federal Assembly, forty-four always
were won by whites because of constituency gerrymandering.

Huggins supported and defended such a distribution of political power. In May 1956 he said:

> We want to indicate to the Africans that provision is made for them to have a place in the sun, as things go along. But we have not the slightest intention of letting them control things until they have proved themselves, and perhaps not even then. That will depend on our grandchildren.[18]

Huggins lived long enough for events to prove him wrong and to demonstrate to him the unpalatable truth that if there was anyone in need of "a place in the sun" it was not the African but the white man. He lived long enough to see the Federation he had so painfully created crumble and the African he had so systematically oppressed come to rule Nyasaland and Northern Rhodesia.

The white man of Central Africa failed to understand the African who was so hostile to paternalism and to the Federation. After all, the Federation increased government spending in Nyasaland and Northern Rhodesia. In Nyasaland, capital and recurrent expenditure had grown by 1958 from $12 million to $33 million; expenditure on roads and buildings had risen by $12 million. Public works expenditure had doubled by 1958 and African civil servants' salaries had risen 78 percent by 1960.[19] The whites argued that the African was benefitting from the Federation. They could not understand why he was so determined to destroy this "far-sighted" scheme in race relations. What the African of Central Africa wanted was to control his own destiny through acquiring political power.

Sir Edgar's Miscalculations

Ever since 1933, when Huggins' conservative Reform Party was elected to power, the European population has tended to reject white liberalism, but since 1958 the trend to conservatism has increased and accelerated. When Sir Edgar

Whitehead became leader of the governing United Federal Party he was not a member of Parliament and therefore could not be the Prime Minister of Rhodesia for more than four months. Under Article 37 of the 1923 Constitution, no minister could hold a portfolio for longer than that period unless he was elected to the Legislative Assembly during that time. In order to conform with this article, Sir Edgar had to be elected to the Assembly before the end of May 1958. J.M. MacDonald, UFP member for Hillside, resigned his seat to allow Sir Edgar to stand for election. This constituency had been considered a safe seat for the government since 1948. On vacating the seat MacDonald said, "I resigned because my constituency is certainly the safest in Matabeleland . . . . I am quite convinced without any shadow of doubt that Sir Edgar will win the seat.[20] He was to be surprised. The more conservative Dominion Party (DP) fielded Jack Graham Pain to oppose Sir Edgar. The by-election was held on April 6, 1958. The Prime Minister of Rhodesia was defeated. The end of the road for white liberalism had been reached; the electorate had indicated that it was looking for a new road, one without any trace of white liberalism. Sir Edgar had no alternative but to appeal to the whole European electorate by requesting the Governor to dissolve the Assembly and call for general elections to be held on June 5, 1958.

Garfield Todd, who had been replaced by Whitehead, and some of his colleagues who had been sacked from office by the more conservative elements of the UFP thought it expedient to move even further to the left on the Rhodesian political spectrum. Todd broke from the UFP and re-established the United Rhodesia Party (URP). In the general elections the DP had thirty candidates, the UFP thirty, the URP twenty-three, and independents two. The Dominion Party, led by professionals with a well-oiled political machine and impressive representatives, enunciated a platform demanding independence for Southern Rhodesia. The Party maintained that political power should remain in the hands of Europeans. The *Rhodesian Herald's* editorial of June 4, 1958, described the DP as "a Party of frightened men." In fact it was not only the DP, but almost every European in Rhodesia, who was frightened of African encroachment on their citadel of political power.

The election had its surprises. The Dominion Party received a plurality of 18,142 votes; the UFP received 16,840, the URP 4,663, and the Independents 67.[21] But the seats had to be redistributed to the parties according to the preferential voting system. According to this system, after voting for his preferred candidate each voter had to cast his second-preference vote, which would be taken into account if there was no candidate with an absolute majority of first-choice votes. As UFP voters exchanged second preference with URP voters, the UFP ended up with seventeen seats in the Legislative Assembly and the DP with thirteen seats. The URP was politically annihilated; Rhodesia had no room for those white elements that sought to appease the African. It must be noted that the preferential voting system was introduced only on October 18, 1957, seven months before the general elections. The UFP government had become alarmed by the successes of the DP and thus had introduced a device to prevent the DP from becoming the government of Rhodesia. If this change had not been adopted the DP would have been elected to power. Nevertheless, these elections to the Ninth Parliament of Rhodesia were a remarkable success for the DP and a warning to the UFP of what might happen and indeed did happen at the next election in 1962.

Although the UFP continued to be the government of Rhodesia after the 1958 elections, Sir Edgar Whitehead was painfully aware of the fact that his party had been returned to power by only 45.1 percent of the votes cast. He was also conscious that the DP was gaining in popularity, as indicated at the polls in 1958. Uppermost in Sir Edgar's mind was the knowledge that the 1958 Todd crisis and its aftermath had been caused by the desire of Todd to accommodate the Africans. And yet he knew that the UFP was being rejected by the European voters and thus had to cultivate support among the bourgeois Africans. He sought to redress the situation, but the

task before him was difficult. To recover the popularity of the
UFP and the government among the Europeans he had to
prove that he was not another Garfield Todd, seemingly willing to appease the Africans. Although he realized that the
European population had irrevocably moved far to the right,
Whitehead needed the African votes to remain in power. He
had to prove to the Africans that he was different from the
leaders of the DP who sought to maintain white supremacy in
Rhodesia.

Whitehead decided to solve this dilemma by maintaining
that the Africans were not interested in politics and that if the
bourgeois Africans could be appeased by what seemed to be
economic and social progress for themselves, he would be able
to get their votes while not alienating the European voters. He
persuaded himself that those who led the African parties were
only power-hungry demagogues who represented nobody.

Whitehead strongly believed that he could also regain the
support of the Europeans of Rhodesia. He was so convinced of
this that he became the victim of his own imagination. In 1961
he thought events had proved him correct. In that year the
Rhodesian electorate had a referendum on whether to accept
the 1961 Draft Constitution. Sir Edgar believed this constitution to be very liberal; when the electorate accepted it by a
margin of 2:1, he thought he had confirmation of European
support.

Actually, the 1961 Constitution was accepted not because
white Rhodesians were becoming more liberal, as Whitehead
thought, but because they were afraid of British intervention
on the African's behalf. According to the 1923 Constitution
Britain could in theory still intervene in Rhodesian affairs
under Sections 28(a) and 31. The whites wanted to be left
alone to deal with the Africans in any way they liked. Thus
they wanted a constitutional conference to write a new constitution for Rhodesia. African representatives were included

in the conference. However, the results of that conference showed how cunning and conspiratory Whitehead's so-called "progressive" government was. They also showed that Britain was prepared to sacrifice the African on the white man's altar. The conference produced a constitution which divided the electorate into "A" roll voters and "B" roll voters. A Legislative Assembly of sixty-five seats was set up, fifty of which were "A" roll and fifteen of which were "B" roll seats. Since few Africans could meet its income, property, and education requirements, eligibility for the "A" roll was almost exclusively limited to white voters. The "B" roll was predominantly black.

Although cross-voting was allowed, when the "B" roll voters voted for candidates for the fifty "A" roll seats, they needed four votes to be equivalent to one "A" roll vote. In other words, four Africans had the same voting weight as one European on the "A" roll. When "A" roll voters voted for candidates for the fifteen "B" roll seats they also needed four votes to be equivalent to one "B" roll vote. But the "A" roll, or white, votes enjoyed an advantage in this cross-voting because, although each "A" roll vote counted as only one quarter when voting for fifteen seats, it counted as one when voting for fifty seats.

The idea was to give the African a token share in the political process. He was allowed fifteen seats in an Assembly of sixty-five. Whitehead was certain that this was all the African wanted. Whitehead was also certain that if the electorate accepted this constitution, he would be assured of European support. During the 1961 referendum campaign he confided to a very close associate of his, A.J.A. Peck: "You know, if we get this Constitution through, the Dominion Party will never be able to get back into power again. It will be finished."[22]

Whitehead was not alone in this belief that the extreme reactionaries among Rhodesia's Europeans had been given a fatal blow in the 1961 referendum. *The Central African Ex-*

aminer, a monthly magazine through which those Europeans who thought they were liberals spoke, shared Whitehead's view. It wrote:

> The referendum result is clearly a tremendous blow to the Dominion Party and, even though their representation in the Legislative Assembly will continue until the new elections are held in fifteen months time, Sir Edgar Whitehead need no longer glance fearfully over his right shoulder before every move he makes.[23]

And indeed Whitehead and his United Federal Party heeded the advice of the *Central African Examiner*. They decided not to look over their right shoulder before every move. They read in the results of the 1961 referendum what they wanted to read—that Rhodesian Europeans were liberal. A. Abrahamson, Sir Edgar's Minister of Labor and Social Welfare, said after the referendum: "Here is our victory; may we use it wisely. Rhodesia has done it again. The moderates of Rhodesia—the very great majority—have done it again."[24]

If the United Federal Party had more carefully analyzed their referendum victory they would have seen that the Europeans did not vote for the Constitution because they were liberal. They voted for it because the Africans were against it. The period between 1960 and the present has seen a development of an acute racial crisis in Rhodesia in which the Europeans regard anything the Africans accept as bad and the Africans regard anything the Europeans accept as bad.

Rejection of Whitehead's Tokenism

Whitehead considered himself a reformer and boasted of having led a liberal government. The reforms he was so proud of include the repeal of the Immorality and Indecency Act, which eliminated the illegality of sexual relations between African men and white women. There was nothing in this "reform" that was in the interest of the majority of the Africans; it served only to offend the white sense of purity. The

Whitehead government was also proud of ending discrimination in swimming baths. The Land Apportionment Act provided that no African could use land in European areas, and therefore no African could swim in the same pool with a white person. For some reason the Whitehead government believed it would be in the interest of the Africans to end such discrimination. The Chief Justice, Sir Hugh Beadle, and Mr. Justice Hathorn ruled in October 1961 that it was illegal under the 1961 Constitution to discriminate against anyone in any public place. Since many swimming baths are such places, this meant that whites would have to see their daughters and wives swim together with "niggers."

One of Whitehead's supporters, Frank Clements, confessed that he could not reconcile Sir Edgar's actions with the European public mood. He wrote:

> I must admit that the popular and official approach to race relations in Southern Rhodesia is evasive and hypocritical. It is not without its irony to note that the firmest "yes" strongholds in the referendum became as bitterly (although a little less abusively) intransigent when the realities of partnership are brought close to their doors. There is certainly some merit in applying the shock treatment to these smug strongholds of political rectitude.

He went on:

> Multiracial bathing is seen by most Europeans in this country to threaten the dignity, chastity and health of the community's young, and above all, of its daughters.[25]

If Whitehead and his UFP had understood the extent to which the Europeans were rejecting Rhodesian liberalism, he might have saved his party and himself from tragic miscalculations. And Sir Edgar's misreading of political moods was even worse when it came to the Africans. What African in Rhodesia would weep because he could not swim with whites? If there were such Africans in 1961 and after, one could count them on the fingers of one hand. Swimming is simply not that important to the average African, and yet the

Whitehead government was priding itself on this great "reform."

In December 1961 the Legislative Assembly of Rhodesia, under the guidance of the Whitehead government, amended the Land Apportionment Act to allow people who marry across the color line to reside in white areas. The government hailed this amendment as a great reform. Again, such a reform did not touch on the grievances of millions of Africans. It catered only to the very few. To the Africans, it was no reform; it was merely another gesture of tokenism.

Africans voiced their rejection of Whitehead's "liberal" gestures most strongly when in their own referendum they rejected the 1961 Constitution. Whitehead regarded them as ungrateful. He could not understand why they would reject a constitution that guaranteed them fifteen seats in an Assembly of sixty-five. To him this constitution was a landmark of white generosity towards the Africans.

Whitehead was completely ignorant of African thinking. What he did not know or perhaps refused to accept was that the African himself was also rejecting white liberalism. To the African, white liberalism had proved oppressive. It was under white liberalism that the Law and Order (Maintenance) Act, the Unlawful Organizations Act, and the Preventive Detention Act—the laws which are used to repress the African parties—were passed. It was under white liberalism that various African parties were banned: the African National Congress in 1959, the National Democratic Party in 1961, and the Zimbabwe African People's Union in 1962. It was under white liberalism that scores of African leaders were rotting in prisons and detention camps. In short, to the African white liberalism meant oppression.

Yet Whitehead had once boasted,

> I know my Africans, and they are not interested in politics. They are interested only in things of immediate practical concern, schools for their children, the improvement of their land, raising their standard of living and things of that kind.[26]

It was these very Africans who, by refusing to support Whitehead in the election of 1962, sent him into retirement, eventually to die in a nursing home for the aged in Britain.

The 1962 Elections

At the end of 1961 the UFP launched a scheme called the Build-A-Nation Campaign in the attempt to win the support of the few Africans who qualified to be either "B" or "A" roll voters. As part of this program, the UFP put into motion the Claim-Your-Vote Campaign, directed mainly to the Africans with a vote. Whitehead believed he would be able to get 50,000 Africans registered as voters. He personally travelled over 3,500 miles in African areas to persuade the African would-be voters to register. But Sir Edgar had completely miscalculated. The Mashonaland organizer of the Build-A-Nation Campaign, a UFP official, revealed in July 1962 that Whitehead's figures were unrealistic. At most, he said, only about 37,000 Africans in the whole of Rhodesia could even qualify to vote.[27]

The UFP completely disregarded the fact that in the unofficial July 1961 referendum held by the African Nationalists, 372,546 Africans had voted against the Constitution, and thus had voted against Sir Edgar and his United Federal Party. Only 471 Africans had voted for the Constitution. If the UFP had taken this unofficial referendum seriously it would probably have discovered the extent to which the Africans were rejecting Rhodesian liberalism. But since Sir Edgar regarded the few Africans who were members of the UFP as the spokesmen for all Africans, he had to await the elections of December 14, 1962 to discover the truth that so many people choose to ignore in Rhodesian politics.

Sir Edgar thought that if he banned the Zimbabwe African People's Union (ZAPU), the sole political vehicle of the Africans in 1962, and restricted the African leaders to their rural homes, he would be able to muster enough African votes to be elected. Thus he banned ZAPU in September 1962. By that time the most reactionary Europeans in Rhodesia had built a very efficient party, the Rhodesia Front, which Sir Edgar also chose to ignore. In fact all the most reactionary groups in Rhodesia—the Rhodesian Ku Klux Klan, the League of Empire Loyalists, the Southern African Alliances, the Southern Rhodesian Association, the Federal Dominion Party, the Southern Rhodesian Dominion Party, and the dissidents of the UFP led by Ian Smith— had begun unity talks immediately after the July 1961 referendum. These organizations at times regarded each other with suspicion and contempt. But as Rhodesia went into the election year they were agreed on one fundamental point: The salvation of white supremacy in Rhodesia lay in their working together. In April 1962 they formed the Rhodesian Front, with cautious Winston Field as its president. Field was chosen for his ability to unite both urban and rural Europeans.

The showdown came on election day. The Africans, mindful that Rhodesian liberalism was as oppressive as Rhodesian reaction, paid heed to the voices of the African leaders calling for an African boycott of the elections. As a result, of the 9,814 African registered voters, only 2,933 voted. The Europeans, realizing that Rhodesian liberalism meant appeasement and tokenism to accommodate the educated Africans, turned out to vote for the Rhodesian Front. When all the votes had been tallied, the Rhodesian Front had won thirty-five seats while the United Federal Party had obtained twenty-nine. The Rhodesian Front became the government of Rhodesia. Rhodesian liberalism had been rejected by both Africans and Europeans.

It is often said by the "liberal" Europeans that it was the Africans who, by their boycott of the elections, elected the Rhodesian Front to power. Indeed there is evidence to prove that had the African "B" roll voters turned out to vote for the UFP European "A" roll candidates, at least five constituencies won by the Rhodesian Front would have been won by the

UFP. This would have put the UFP back into power. The critical constituencies were the Matobo, Bulawayo District, Eastern, Marandellas, and Mazoe.

But what these disappointed "liberals" forget is that the Africans already had proof of the oppressiveness of the UFP, and they had further proof that the RF would be oppressive if elected. There was nothing to choose between the UFP and the RF. To say this is not to say it was wise for Africans to boycott the 1962 elections. The mistake of the African leaders was to call for the boycott of the elections without any plan to put into effect after the boycott. Since the boycott was not part of a plan but an isolated event which did not require much thought and effort to carry out, it did not have much effect in Rhodesian politics. This was tragic.

The elections of 1962 ended a long era of deception under a form of liberalism designed to prevent Africans from exercising political power in the land of their birth. The elections ushered in a period of honest reaction based on the realistic political forces and philosophies that operate in Rhodesia. Ian Douglas Smith, the Prime Minister of Rhodesia since April 1964, is a sincere man. He believes in reaction and the superiority of the white man, and he puts this philosophy into practice.

NOTES

1. Keatley, *Politics*, p. 292.

2. E. Tawse-Jolie, *The Real Rhodesia* (London: Hutchinson & Co., 1924), pp. 48–49.

3. Keatley, *Politics*, p. 294.

4. *Ibid., p. 295.*

5. *Theodore Bull, Crisis of Color: Rhodesia* (Chicago: Quadrangle Books, 1967), p. 16.

6. R. Gray, *The Two Nations* (Oxford: Oxford University Press, 1960), p. 232.

7. See Keatley, *Politics*, p. 437.

8. *Rhodesia Herald*, July 22, 1960.

9. See *The Daily News* (Salisbury) of July 8, 20–30, 1960, and the *Rhodesia Herald* (Salisbury) of July 8, 20–30, 1960.

10. "Whitehead's Short Term Victories," *Central African Examiner*, August 1961.

11. Keatley, *Politics*, p. 263.

12. *The Tredgold Commission Report*, Salisbury, 1957.

13. *Ibid.*

14. Kenneth D. Kaunda, *Zambia Shall be Free* (New York: Praeger, 1962).

15. Roy Welensky, *4000 Days* (London: Collins, 1964).

16. The Federation of Rhodesia and Nyasaland was officially dissolved on December 31, 1963.

17. The Federation of Rhodesia and Nyasaland, Voters Roll, Salisbury, 1962.

18. Keatley, *Politics*, p. 224.

19. Reg Heath, *Year Book and Guide of the Rhodesias and Nyasaland* (Salisbury: Rhodesian Publications, 1960), pp. 59–64.

20. *Rhodesian Herald*, February 24, 1958.

21. Collin Leys, *European Politics in Southern Rhodesia* (London: Praeger, 1960), p. 310.

22. A.J.A. Peck, *Rhodesia Accuses* (Salisbury: Three Sisters, 1966), p. 111. Sir Edgar speaks as if the Dominion Party had actually been in power in Rhodesia. This statement betrays his frightened state of mind which was conceding the victory to the DP in the election of 1958 although the DP was prevented from assuming power.

23. "The Birth of a Nation?" *Central African Examiner*, August 1961.

24. *The Bulawayo Chronicle*, July 27, 1961.

25. Frank Clements, "Too Deep a Plunge," *Central African Examiner*, September 1961.

26. Keatley, *Politics*, p. 219.

27. M.A. Pedder, "No Claim Bonus," *Central African Examiner*, March 1962.

28. *Central African Examiner*, July 1962.

CHAPTER 3

UDI and Responses

During the 1962 election campaign, the Rhodesian Front (RF) promised the electorate that it would lead Rhodesia to independence under white rule by any means available. This was not just an election gimmick, because the rank and file of the party expected their leaders to redeem this promise. Thus Winston Field, the leader of the RF and the Prime Minister of Rhodesia, began demanding Rhodesia's independence from Britain immediately after he had assumed office. The British Conservative government under Sir Alec Douglas-Home requested him to prove beyond any doubt that all races in the country supported his demand. It was easy for the RF to prove that it had the support of the Europeans—since it had been elected to power on the platform of independence. The problem was to show that the Africans, the Asians, and the Coloreds (racially mixed) supported his demand. Field decided to consult African chiefs on the question, but the British government indicated that it did not consider the chiefs to be representative of the Africans. Britian recognized the two African parties—the Zimbabwe African National Union (ZANU) and the Zimbabwe African People's Union (ZAPU)—as the spokesmen of the African People.

The position taken by the British government led to a deadlock on the question of independence. The RF began thinking of declaring independence unilaterally, i.e., without Britain's consent. Field considered such a course of action suicidal and treasonous. But some members of his cabinet, like Deputy Prime Minister Ian Smith, thought that such a rebellion would just be a "three day wonder," with people soon growing accustomed to the idea. In October 1963, Field made his position clear: "We shall continue to negotiate, but we are not prepared to go to the extent of handing over authority to those [the Africans] as yet unfitted and untrained to wield it."[1] In February 1964 he again announced that he would continue to negotiate for independence. RF members of Parliament seethed with dissatisfaction over the way Field was handling the independence issue. The Front wanted a ruthless and fearless leader who would get independence by any means. In April 1964 the question of leadership came to a head. The majority of cabinet ministers no longer had confidence in Field. They brought the question of leadership to the Rhodesian Front caucus.

Ian Douglas Smith, the Deputy Leader, was elected to replace Field as leader of the RF and Prime Minister of Rhodesia. He was given the task of leading Rhodesia to independence. Smith's first objective was to build a popular base in the RF and to deliver a fatal blow to European opposition in Parliament; he would use the device of elections and referenda to attain this objective. The second objective was to wipe out African opposition; he would use repression to accomplish this goal.

RF Consolidation and Elimination
of European Oppositon

The best method of consolidating the political base of the Rhodesian Front from which the Unilateral Declaration of Independence (UDI) would be launched was to whip up the emotions of the Europeans by appealing to their racial instincts and fears. By-elections were deemed a suitable instrument for this. The first opportunity to offer itself to Smith was the death of Harry Roberts, a Rhodesian Front member of Parliament. In the 1962 elections Roberts had won the Matobo Constituency by a small majority of thirty-four votes, with 61 percent of the constituency voting. Both the Rhodesian Front and the European opposition party, the United Federal Party, regarded the by-election for his vacant seat as a test of strength between the two parties. By the time the by-election was held in May 1963, the United Federal Party had changed its name to the Rhodesia National Party (RNP). But the leadership remained the same.

The campaign for this by-election was a bitter one. While the two parties were contesting this one seat in Parliament, their eyes were set on a larger issue—independence. Like its leader, Sir Edgar Whitehead, the RNP vacillated on the independence issue, while the RF frankly stated that it had one purpose—solely to look after European interests. The RF declared that only the interests of the white man of Rhodesia would dictate the methods it would use to acquire independence. The whites of Rhodesia responded and the RF candidate, S. A. Wilmont, won the Matobo by-election by a majority of 271 votes. The by-election proved one point: Contrary to press reports, by May 1963 the RF had grown more popular with Europeans than it had been in December 1962. The African voters in the Matobo Constituency took part in the by-election. Only 59 had voted in the 1962 elections, but 196 voted in the 1963 by-election and all except two voted for the RNP candidate. But still the RF candidate won by an increased majority. There was a 15 percent European vote swing from the RNP to the RF and the turnout of the African voters could not upset this swing.[2]

The RNP became very disillusioned by this defeat, not because it had failed to win the by-election, but because the defeat revealed that the whites of Rhodesia had put their faith in the RF. A number of the members of the RNP began to resign from the party, either to join the RF bandwagon or to remain uncommitted.

One year after the 1963 by-election the RNP began to discuss ways of reorganizing itself. While these discussions were going on, Speaker of the House Dr. Walter Alexander died. The RF was eager to have another by-election to test its strength again. Thus the RF refused to let one of its members of Parliament be elected to the position of Speaker of the House. In Rhodesia, as in Britain, the Speaker of the House is non-political and does not represent any constituency, yet he must be elected from among the members of Parliament. The RNP was persuaded to stand one of its own members of Parliament for election to the position of Speaker. Rube Stumbles was elected Speaker and had to resign his seat for the Avondale Constituency. At almost the same time, B.V. Ewing, another RNP member of Parliament, sensing the trend of events and opinion in Rhodesia, resigned his seat for the Arundale Constituency to go into business. Thus two by-elections had to be held and the RF was elated at these opportunities. The two by-elections were set for October 1, 1964.

The RNP was nervous and no longer sure what was happening. It decided to dissolve itself in August 1964 and call Sir Roy Welensky, at one time the charismatic Prime Minister of the Federation of Rhodesia and Nyasaland, to form a new party. Sir Roy came out of retirement to form the Rhodesia Party (RP) with Sir Edgar Whitehead as the Deputy Leader. The former Rhodesia National Party members congregated under these two men. Sir Roy himself decided to contest the Arundale seat, and the RP picked a prominent man, Sydney Sawyer, to contest the Avondale seat. Both constituencies had been safe for the RNP and were presumed safe for the RP. The Rhodesian Front regarded these two by-elections as being of very great importance in measuring its own popularity. Ian Smith himself had wanted to resign his Umzingwane seat and oppose Sir Roy in Arundale. But the RF decided that the Deputy Prime Minister, Clifford Dupont, should resign his

Charter constituency seat and oppose Sir Roy in Arundale. The Rhodesian Front was not sacrificing Dupont; its intention was to test the popularity of the party. The RF reasoned that if Dupont were defeated in Arundale he could stand for election in his old Charter constituency in a by-election, but to whip up the voters Dupont announced that if he were defeated in the Arundale by-election he would not seek re-election anywhere else. For the Avondale constituency the RF ran J.W. Pithey, a former Secretary of Justice, against the RP's Sydney Sawyer.

The campaign in these two by-elections was vicious and took on tones that had never been known in Rhodesian elections. The RF Youth Wing disrupted RP election meetings. Sir Roy was called "a Communist," "a traitor," "a bloody Jew," "a coward."[3] The Rhodesian Front platform proposed that Rhodesia must have its independence under the 1961 Constitution. The Front declared that Unilateral Declaration of Independence was not an election issue, because its goal was to obtain independence through negotiation. During this campaign Smith flew to London in September 1964. This gave the electorate the impression that the Front was sincerely working towards getting independence through negotiations. The RP was accused of splitting the Europeans at a time when the Prime Minister was negotiating for independence. While Smith was in London, the British government repeated that it would give Rhodesia independence if Smith could show that he had the support of both Europeans and Africans. The RF used this condition as a campaign weapon. It called upon the electorate to show that it was behind the Prime Minister in his negotiations for independence.

The RP found its position terribly weakened. It opposed a Unilateral Declaration of Independence but failed to prove that the RF had such intentions. The RP said that its intention was to get independence through negotiation, yet it appeared as if this was exactly what the RF was trying to do. The RP announced in its Statement of Policy, No. 4, that it would "repeal the appropriate sections of the Land Apportionment Act until it is completely phased out of existence."[4] No. 2 in the same Statement of Policy read as follows: "The Rhodesia Party will make no change in the 'A' roll franchise but consideration will be given to some changes in the 'B' roll franchise for the special purpose of bringing older Africans on this roll."[5] The RP seemed not to have learned a lesson from its predecessor, the UFP of 1962; such statements during electioneering could only destroy the image of the party among the Europeans. It cannot be said that the statements were put out to woo African votes, because the Arundale and Avondale constituencies are exclusively white suburbs and therefore without any African votes.

On October 1, 1964, both Sir Roy and Sydney Sawyer were soundly defeated by the RF candidates. The RF was able to convert UFP majorities in the elections of 1962 into its own majorities in the by-elections of 1964. The RF was consolidating its position and mobilizing European support. Sir Roy accepted the obvious and went back into retirement. Sir Edgar, still refusing to give in, assumed the leadership of the Rhodesia Party.

The Rhodesian Front victory in the Arundale and Avondale by-elections heralded the extinction of the Rhodesia Party. The RF was confident of its policies and the line it was taking. It now wanted to show the British government and the world that the electorate was behind it in its demand for independence under the 1961 Constitution. Ian Smith and his colleagues also wanted to exploit to the fullest extent the rising emotions of the Europeans. Immediately after the by-elections, the RF government scheduled a referendum for November 5, 1964. The question posed to the voters was, "Do you want independence under the 1961 Constitution?" The question did not state how the independence was to be obtained. The RP was caught without a platform; the nature of the question allowed it no alternative. Thus it decided not to give any directives on how its supporters were to vote and said only that they should vote according to their consciences. It found itself completely outmaneuvered by the RF.

The RP's refusal to take active part in the referendum campaign tended to throw its supporters into the outstretched arms of the RF. As a result, all the constituencies voted overwhelmingly for independence under the 1961 Constitution. It was only a matter of time before the RP and any form of European opposition to the RF disappeared completely from the Rhodesian political scene. Immediately after the referendum the RP removed Whitehead from leadership and replaced him with David Butler, an inexperienced young man. Sir Edgar became the scapegoat for the failures of the RP, which refused to accept the fact that its failures were the result of its misreading of the Rhodesian political climate.

The difficulties of the RP did not pass unnoticed by the RF, which was looking for a pretext to wipe European oppositon from the political scene. But Ian Smith knew that he could not lock all the leaders of the European opposition in his jails without losing the political ground he had gained and so much needed for his Unilateral Declaration of Independence. Thus he wanted the electorate itself to do the job. Scarcely before David Butler had consolidated his position as the new leader of the RP, Smith announced in April 1965 that he had advised the Governor to dissolve the Tenth Parliament, which had lived only half of its five-year term, and call for general elections on May 7, 1965. The period between the announcement of the general elections and the date for the elections was the shortest possible time permissible under the Electoral Act. Moreover, the electoral roll was completely out of date; some voters had left the country, others had died, and yet they were still on the roll, while many voters had changed their addresses. These discrepancies did not bother the RF. They only wanted the European electorate to help them deliver a *coup de grâce* to the European opposition.

The RP found it extremely difficult to prepare for these elections. It could not locate voters and could find men and women to stand for elections in only twenty-five of the fifty "A" roll constituencies. Three other Europeans stood for elections in "A" roll constituencies as independents. Thus the RF approached the election day with twenty-two candidates unopposed. The RP had found fifteen Africans to contest all the "B" roll seats. The RF decided not to contest the "B" roll seats because it feared that a defeat of its "B" roll candidates would belie its contention that Africans supported it.

By election day most political observers in Rhodesia had accepted the obvious—that the RF would be returned to power with an increased comfortable majority in Parliament. But no one ever dreamed that every European "A" roll candidate opposing the RF would be defeated. By winning every "A" roll seat available, the RF had completely wiped out the last vestige of organized European opposition in Rhodesia and paved the way for a unilateral declaration of independence. What further surprised political observers and encouraged the RF was the extent of the European vote swing from the RP to the RF. An examination of the twenty-eight "A" roll constituencies in which there were contests in both the 1962 and 1965 elections reveals that on the average there was a 30 percent vote swing to the Rhodesian Front.[6] No one could dispute the claim of the RF that it had overwhelming European support.

The Elimination of African Opposition

The Rhodesian Front used planning and political manuevering to deal with European oppositon. Its approach to African oppositon was very simple and direct and required no political finesse. The Front's approach to African opposition was guided by its belief that "the African gravitates to the stronger" and that "the crack of the whip" is what he understands best and in the long run appreciates.[7]

As soon as the RF came to power in December 1962 it began to tighten security laws in preparation for suppressing the Africans and eliminating them as a political force. By April 1963 the House had passed the Preservation of Constitutional Government Act, whose Section II imposed a penalty of up to twenty years on conviction for any subversive activities carried on outside the country against Rhodesia. This Act was supposed to be examined by the Constitutional Council, which under the 1961 Constitution was to be the watchdog for any unconstitutional act by the government. But Prime Minister Winston Field invoked the powers given him by the 1961 Constitution to side-step the Council by issuing a Certificate of Urgency. This allowed passage of the bill without any examination by the Constitutional Council.

The RF government became more vicious in 1964. The Minister of Law and Order, Clifford Dupont, scrupulously applied the Law and Order (Maintenance) Act that had been passed by the UFP government. Dupont revealed in Parliament that on February 27, 1964, there were thirty-eight people below the age of seventeen and ten between the ages of seventeen and nineteen detained and awaiting trial. Eight of them had been held for more than twenty-eight days and three had been held for three months or longer without trial. On March 4, 1964 eleven juveniles charged under the Act were refused bail and were remanded into custody until March 17. Three were girls between the ages of fourteen and sixteen, and one was a girl of twelve. In March Dupont revealed that some seventeen-year-old boys were serving sentences of six years with hard labor and that fifteen boys of the same age were serving sentences of up to sixteen years with hard labor.[8] Section 44 of the Law and Order (Maintenance) Act was amended to increase the restriction period from three to twelve months, and a section was inserted that provided a mandatory death penalty for any person convicted of throwing explosives or bombs (or both) at any building or property that could be occupied by persons. Throughout 1963 and part of 1964 when these Draconian laws were being passed, the UFP could not oppose them because the RF government was following a UFP beaten track. After all, it was the UFP that had enacted most of these laws the RF was now "improving."

In the face of this "iron rod" administration, the Zimbabwe African People's Union split from top to bottom in 1963, as will be discussed in Chapter 6. The two factions, the Zimbabwe African National Union (ZANU) and the People's Caretaker Council (PCC), began bickering with each other, inciting their followers to liquidate physically the supporters of the other faction. The RF government welcomed and even encouraged this infighting between the two nationalist factions. For example, it reduced the strength of the police force in the African townships so that the African people could suffer to the greatest extent possible from the fighting between the factions. One year of chaos was allowed to take hold of African townships. When the government was satisfied that the African nationalists had done enough havoc on their own people, it banned the two factions and detained the leaders. All the operational cells of the African nationalists were uprooted and destroyed.

Thus, the second objective of the RF was attained. Indeed the RF had liquidated African opposition a year before it had completely liquidated European opposition.

By May 8, 1965 the road was clear for the RF. The African leaders were safely locked in jail or behind fences in detention camps, and the European opposition had been annihilated at the polls. Ian Smith and his cohorts were now ready to deal with Britain.

The Challenge of UDI

After the 1965 elections most Europeans in Rhodesia adopted the attitude of "I will support my country, right or wrong." The RF exploited this state of mind and assured the Europeans that it would obtain independence for them. On October 9, 1965, Ian Smith repeated that Britain's terms were unacceptable to the Rhodesians. While he was still in London he said that Rhodesians "would rather go down fighting than crawling on hands and knees" and added,

I think we may have made up our minds already. I will be going home for a final decision on this and I do not believe it will take long. . . . We are prepared to take a chance. We take it with our eyes open. . . . It would be terrible and unfortunate if, through being faint-hearted, we were frightened out of what we are doing and if we lost our country simply because we did not stand up for it. If we stand up for it we may win everything we are looking for.[9]

Even after this ominous warning some people in Rhodesia and Britain thought Smith was bluffing. After all, Field had done the same talking. They underestimated Smith's strong personality and principles. Smith had built himself into a charismatic leader and won the support of Europeans. A type of McCarthyism had developed in Rhodesia, so that to oppose Smith seemed communistic. Even those who were opposed to the Unilateral Declaration of Independence feared to speak out against it. Only a few industrialists spoke out against the rebellion.

Although at first British Prime Minister Harold Wilson thought that Smith was bluffing, by October 1965 he realized the intensity of the situation. He wanted to save it if he could and flew to Rhodesia to dissuade Smith from the path he was following. He spent over nine hours in discussion with the Rhodesian government and twenty-nine hours talking with leaders of all sections of Rhodesian life. Before he left Rhodesia he acknowledged that

there can be no doubt, I am afraid, that the situation is hyper-charged with emotion. And this is not conducive to getting the right answer. For among those emotions, predominant is the emotion of fear, with attendant emotions of distrust and suspicion and of unfounded rumor. . . . To adapt the words of President Roosevelt, the first freedom that Rhodesia needs to achieve, the foundation of all the others, is freedom from fear.[10]

Britain made a point of telling the Europeans of Rhodesia that it would not meet the challenge of UDI with force. While in Salisbury, Wilson assured the would-be rebels by saying,

> If there are those who are thinking in terms of a thunderbolt hurtling from the sky and destroying their enemies, a thunderbolt in the shape of the Royal Air Force, let me say that thunderbolt will not be coming . . . and to continue in this delusion wastes valuable time and misdirects valuable energies.[11]

In a speech in the British House of Commons Wilson later reiterated the position of his government that it would not use any military force to suppress the UDI.

Smith found himself in a position he had never dreamed of. He was the master in Rhodesia, and Britain was bowing to him, although it was threatening economic sanctions. He knew that with the overwhelming support of the Rhodesian Europeans behind him and with the assurance from Britain that force would not be used, he would be a fool not to carry out the rebellion for which he had so cunningly worked for over a year. He further knew that if he failed to carry out the rebellion he would be signing his political death warrant. Most of his cabinet colleagues and most rural branches of the RF expected the Declaration of Independence on the date unofficially indicated by Smith, October 17, 1965. Smith was able to postpone it only because he argued that since Wilson wanted to come to Rhodesia at the end of October it was imperative for Rhodesia that the UDI be put off for a few days. After the Wilson visit, Smith decided to throw down the gauntlet. On November 11, 1965 at 1:15 P.M., Smith —using almost the same language as the American Declaration of Independence—unilaterally declared Rhodesia independent from Britain.[12]

African Lack of Response

The factional fighting between the People's Caretaker Council and the Zimbabwe African National Union in 1963 and 1964 had demoralizing effects on the African people of Zimbabwe. They saw brother turn against brother, and they could not understand it. It was at this time, when African morale was at its lowest, that Smith unilaterally declared Rhodesia independent. The Africans could not unite against Smith. There were scattered acts of violence which were quickly suppressed by the regime. During the infighting between PCC and ZANU the African nationalists had forgotten that the white man in Rhodesia was the enemy and hence had not built a revolutionary infrastructure to oppose UDI. This lack of African response to UDI further demoralized the African people. Although the Africans in exile attempted to wage a guerrilla war against Rhodesia, the war was misconceived and misdirected for reasons that will be discussed in the following chapters.

British Inaction

The British government was caught unprepared by the UDI. Despite the fact that the Rhodesian Front government had threatened UDI since 1962, the British government doubted that people of British stock would rebel against the British Crown. The only such rebellion had been the American revolt in 1775. When the unexpected occurred and Smith went ahead with his rebellion, Britain could not militarily move against its kith and kin in Rhodesia. It devised an impotent policy of economic sanctions as a response to UDI. In two separate studies, I have reviewed in detail the reactions of Britain to UDI and the whole policy of economic sanctions against Rhodesia.[13] To summarize here, Britain was not politically and economically equipped to apply economic sanctions against Rhodesia. The Labor Party, which was the government of Britain when UDI was declared, had a majority of only four in the House of Commons and was about to call for general elections. Prime Minister Wilson was fearful that a vigorous policy against Rhodesia would alienate the British voters who were blood relatives of the Rhodesian whites.

Economically, Britain had an unfavorable balance of payments and a deficit of two and one-quarter billion dollars. Unemployment was rife, and prices were going up at a rapid rate. This was not the economy that could sustain leadership in any implementation and enforcement of economic sanctions. Britain was unwilling to undertake any exercise that would further weaken its economy, and the Labor Government was unwilling to take any action that might lead it to defeat either on the floor of the House of Commons or at the electoral polls.

These political and economic considerations led to British reluctance to recommend to the United Nations Security Council comprehensive economic sanctions against Rhodesia immediately after UDI had been effected. Instead, in November 1965 Britain recommended undesignated voluntary economic sanctions. With the support of its Western allies and the indifference of the socialist states towards the Rhodesian crisis, Britain suceeded in having the Security Council accept its recommendation.

By December 1966 Britain realized how impotent the voluntary economic sanctions were. Thus it recommended selective mandatory economic sanctions, and the Security Council accepted. But the Security Council sanction resolution had too many loopholes to be effective; moreover, some paragraphs were subject to more than one interpretation.[14] A year and a half after the application of selective economic sanctions the Rhodesian regime was still firmly in control. In May 1968 Britain, pressured by the Afro-Asian states, recommended comprehensive economic sanctions against Rhodesia.[15] By that time the Rhodesian regime had reorganized its economy by diversifying it and producing substitutes for its imports. It had also completed the organization of its clandestine trade.

OAU Exercise in Futility

The response of the world to UDI and the policy of economic sanctions against Rhodesia was varied. The Organization of African Unity, OAU, though in sympathy with the people of Zimbabwe, adopted an exercise in futility as its response to the Rhodesian crisis. On December 2, 1965, the OAU Council of Ministers met to devise the African response to UDI. It recommended to the African heads of states that if Britain failed to end UDI in Rhodesia by December 15, 1965, the African states should sever diplomatic relations with Britain.[16] But when by the appointed date Britain had neither taken nor shown that it intended to take vigorous and effective measures against the Rhodesian rebel regime, only ten African states out of thirty-six actually implemented the OAU resolution. President Julius Nyerere of Tanzania, disgusted with African disregard of their own resolution asked, "Do African States meet in solemn conclave to make noise? Or do they mean what they say?" He went on to say, "If we ignore our own resolution, neither our suffering brothers in Rhodesia, in Mozambique, in Angola, in South Africa, in South West Africa nor the broad masses of people of Africa, nor for that matter the non-members of the United Nations Organization could ever trust Africa to honor a pledge solemnly undertaken by Africa's leaders."[17] African states had shown that they had arrived at their decision to break diplomatic and economic relations with Britain without having examined their capability to do so.

Realities and Conspiracy in Central and Southern Africa

The historical, political, and economic relationships of the countries in Central and Southern Africa made the responses of Zambia, Malawi, and Botswana to the Rhodesian rebellion difficult and painful. At the same time they reinforced the conspiracy between Rhodesia, South Africa, and "Portuguese" Mozambique.

When the Federation of Rhodesia and Nyasaland, comprising the three British territories of Southern Rhodesia, Northern Rhodesia, and Nyasaland, was created in 1953 the supporters of the scheme in both Central Africa and Britain advanced the theory that it would make the economies of these territories more viable.[18] Southern Rhodesia turned out to be the focal point of the Federation. Northern Rhodesia and Nyasaland became markets for Southern Rhodesian manufactured products and sources of cheap labor for Southern Rhodesian agricultural and mining. Copper, the chief export of Northern Rhodesia, was dispatched by the Rhodesia Railways through Southern Rodesia to the seaport of Beira in Mozambique. Northern Rhodesia received the coal needed for its copper industry from Southern Rhodesia and was discouraged from exploring its own coal resources on the grounds that it would be expensive. Imports to Northern Rhodesia went by rail from Beira through Southern Rhodesia; the power plant of the giant Kariba hydroelectric dam, which provided Southern Rhodesia and Northern Rhodesia with electricity, was built on Southern Rhodesian territory. Northern Rhodesia was discouraged from developing a hydroelectric scheme on the Kafue River. The University College of Rhodesia and Nyasaland was built in Salisbury, the capital of both Rhodesia and the Federation. In short, Southern Rhodesia became the nerve center of the Federation of Rhodesia and Nyasaland.

The Federation of Rhodesia and Nyasaland was dissolved in 1963; Nyasaland attained its independence and became Malawi, and Northern Rhodesia became Zambia the following year. But their economies had become so integrated with Rhodesia's that the economic survival of the two new nations was dependent on Rhodesia.

The Zambezi River, the boundary between Zambia and Rhodesia, became a battle line of two conflicting political ideologies; the Rhodesia Front, the governing party of Rhodesia, believed in white supremacy, while Zambia's governing United National Independence Party believed in Pan Africanism and the right of the majority to self-determination. South Africa, dedicated to its policy of apartheid, was in sympathy with Rhodesia. Portugal, the administering authority of Mozambique constantly harassed by Mozambique nationalist movements, was also sympathetic to Rhodesia. Malawi, under the Malawi Congress Party, refrained from declaring its attitude towards Rhodesia, South Africa, and Portugal. Bechuanaland was governed by the British until it became the independent Republic of Botswana in October 1966.

At the time of UDI, Zambia imported from Rhodesia goods worth almost $100 million a year—about 40 percent of its total imports. Zambia received nearly 80 percent of its requirements of manufactured goods from Rhodesia and depended wholly on Rhodesia for its clothing requirements.[19] Most of Zambia's coal was obtained from Rhodesia; its oil came from the Central African Petroleum Refinery, Ltd., in Umtali, Rhodesia; and the Kariba hydroelectric project, whose plant is under Rhodesian authority, provided Zambia with most of its electric power requirements.[20] At the time of UDI Zambia's economic dependence on Rhodesia was well established.

At the time of UDI Malawi imported from Rhodesia goods valued at almost $21 million annually and exported to Rhodesia goods worth close to $4.5 million.[21] Malawi wholly depended on Rhodesia for its meat and meat products, sugar, manufactured products, and coal. The transport of goods from Rhodesia to Malawi was subsidized by Rhodesian wholesalers. A number of industrial and commercial firms in Malawi operated from a Rhodesian base and depended for their funds on Rhodesian firms and banks. The Air Malawi route between Blantyre and Salisbury provided Malawi with about $450,000 annually. At the time of UDI about 300,000 Malawian citizens were working on Rhodesian farms and in Rhodesian mines, and this was said to be relieving Malawi's unemployment problems.

The overseas exports and imports of Malawi were transported through Beira in Mozambique. A railway line directly connects Malawi and Beira, and Rhodesia loaned Malawi part of the rolling stock needed for the transportation of the goods.

Thus, the goodwill of both Portugal and Rhodesia was necessary for the economic survival of Malawi.

When Botswana attained its independence in October 1966, goods from Rhodesia made up 23.4 percent of its total imports—almost $6 million—and goods sent to Rhodesia made up 17.1 percent of its exports—close to $2.5 million.[22] Furthermore, Botswana's exports to other African countries pass through Rhodesia and are transported for that part of the journey by the Rhodesia Railway lines. Cattle constitute seven-eighths of these exports, and cattle ranching occupies 90 percent of Botswana's labor force; seventy-five percent of cattle transportation within Botswana is also supplied by the Rhodesia Railways. Botswana's econony heavily relies on the Rhodesia Railways, and the only outlets of Botswana to the sea are Portuguese and South African ports.

Before the imposition of economic sanctions, Rhodesia's overseas exports and imports went by rail through the port of Beira. The crude oil for Rhodesia was carried by a ten-inch, 184-mile pipeline that connected Beira with the Central African Petroleum Refinery at Umtali. The pipeline is owned by the Companhia do Pipeline Moçambique-Rhodesia, in which British and Portuguese subsidiaries hold interests; Portugal holds the majority of the votes on the company's Board of Directors. Thus the port of Beira was of great importance to the economy of Rhodesia. The other Rhodesian outlet to the sea is the port of Lourenço Marques, also in Mozambique. In order for Rhodesia to use this port, goods have to be transported by road to Messina in South Africa and then by rail to Lourenço Marques. Since both Beira and Lourenço Marques are in the Portuguese territory of Mozambique the attitude of Portugal to Rhodesia was of great significance in determining the extent to which Rhodesia would survive economic sanctions.

Trade between Mozambique and Rhodesia was not very high before UDI. In 1965 Rhodesia exported to Mozambique goods valued at little more than $3 million and imported from

Mozambique goods worth $3 million; this is only about 0.75 percent of Rhodesia's total exports and imports.[23] Thus in terms of real trade Mozambique was not of any economic value to Rhodesia. It was its geographical position that made it so important.

But the trade between South Africa and Rhodesia was fairly large at the time of UDI. Rhodesia imported from South Africa goods worth $77.5million, or 26 percent of Rhodesia's imports. Considering the size of Rhodesia's economy, this is a fairly high level of imports from one country. Only the United Kingdom provided Rhodesia with more goods than South Africa before UDI.[24] In 1965 Rhodesia exported to South Africa goods worth almost $41 million, or about 10 percent of Rhodesia's total exports. South Africa was the third largest of Rhodesia's markets, after Zambia and Britain.

South Africa, with a strong economy, occupied a strategic position which could determine the effectiveness of economic sanctions against Rhodesia. If South Africa had decided to apply economic sanctions the chances for Rhodesia to survive them would have been slim. But South Africa chose to assist Rhodesia, and Rhodesia was able to survive the sanctions. South Africa's economy was strong enough to stand the effects of Rhodesia's trade slipping into the world economy through South Africa.

After UDI it was to Rhodesia's advantage to preserve the pattern of economic relations that existed in Central and Southern Africa. Zambia, Malawi, Botswana, Mozambique, and South Africa together bought about 42 percent of Rhodesia's exports and provided about a third of Rhodesia's imports. The Rhodesian Front government knew that both South Africa and Portugal shared its desire to preserve white supremacy. They also shared the common discomfort of attacks by African nationalists fighting to achieve majority rule in their respective territories. Since Rhodesia's rebellion against Britain was prosecuted in defense of white supremacy Rhodesia calculated that, although South Africa and Portugal had advised against UDI, presented with a *fait accompli* they would rally to Rhodesia's support.

Furthermore, both South Africa and Portugal shared Rhodesia's contempt for the United Nations, which Britain had requested to support the economic sanctions against Rhodesia. South Africa and Portugal had been condemned year after year by the United Nations for their oppressive policies. If economic sanctions were to succeed against Rhodesia, the chances for their being used against South Africa and Portugal would be increased. Thus they shared Rhodesia's desire to frustrate economic sanctions and expose their futility as a weapon of United Nations action.

Nearly a year before UDI, on November 30, 1964, Rhodesia and South Africa signed a five-year trade agreement effective December 1, 1964, to December 31, 1969, and to continue thereafter unless either party gave twelve months' notice of termination. The agreement allowed for the entry of Rhodesian manufactured products into South Africa either duty free or at a preferential rate. Rhodesia was attempting to find a market in South Africa for the products which it traditionally exported to Zambia and Malawi, as it suspected that the former would apply economic sanctions against it and feared that the latter might do the same under international pressure. Rhodesia regarded Botswana with outright contempt, considering it incapable of effectively applying economic sanctions.

In September 1964 Ian Smith, passing through Portugal on his way to London, reminded Prime Minister Salazar and his Foreign Minister Franco Nogueira that Portugal was one of Rhodesia's "oldest and most trusted allies and friends in the world."[25] In July 1965 Rhodesia announced that Harry Reedman would be its accredited diplomatic representative to Portugal and John Gaunt its representative to South Africa. Reedman took his office in September 1965, after much diplomatic effort by Britain to block the appointment. The British position was that Rhodesia was not a sovereign country and could not have an accredited diplomatic representative in a foreign country; Rhodesia's representation in foreign countries was to be attached to the British embassies. Gaunt and Reedman prepared South Africa and Portugal for Rhodesia's Unilateral Declaration of Independence in November 1965 and ensured their support of Rhodesia in the economic warfare that followed.

South African and Mozambican commercial documents, indicating the origin of goods, have been issued and signed by appropriate South African and Mozambique officials to cover up Rhodesian goods evading the sanctions. The embargoed goods have safely found their way into world market— including British markets. Imports from all over the world, ostensibly bought by South African companies and at times by bogus companies purportedly in existence in South Africa, are re-exported to Rhodesia. Despite the imposition of selective mandatory economic sanctions in December 1966 and of comprehensive mandatory economic sanctions in May 1968, Rhodesia managed to export $264 million worth of goods in 1967 and $256 million worth of goods in 1968. In 1967 it imported $262 million worth of goods and in 1968 $290 million.[26] South Africa and Portugal had come to the rescue of Rhodesia.

Led by Dr. Kenneth Kaunda, one of the most sincere political leaders Africa has ever had, Zambia adopted the position, from its inception as an independent nation, that the regimes in Mozambique, Rhodesia, and South Africa are oppressive and despicable on moral grounds. It advocated international action through the United Nations to put an end to the oppressive regimes. In particular, Zambia urged Britain to take military action to prevent Rhodesia's Unilateral Declaration of Independence.

When Britain went to the United Nations requesting economic sanctions against Rhodesia, Zambia held that because of South Africa's strategic position a program of economic sanctions against Rhodesia would fail. President

Kaunda tirelessly urged Britain, to no avail, to use force in Rhodesia to end the rebellion. Kaunda allowed Zambia to serve as the host country to liberation movements waging guerrilla warfare against the Southern African regimes.

Zambia is on the front line of the battle between Pan Africanism and white supremacy. Its own internal policies of building one nation are constantly put to the test as the tensions in Rhodesia affect race relations in Zambia itself. Since its economy at the time of UDI was so dependent on Rhodesia, it was open to retaliatory action by Rhodesia. There was even the possibility of being held hostage in the economic warfare between the United Nations and Rhodesia, for Rhodesia hoped that the UN would mitigate its sanctions against it if Zambia could also be made victim of them.

The Zambian government responded favorably to the United Nations call to apply economic sanctions—despite economic harm the country would suffer. But many companies which operated in Zambia were offshoots of Rhodesian-based companies and were reluctant to enforce the sanction measures. At first the Zambian Ministry of Commerce, Industry, and Foreign Trade urged the companies to seek alternative sources of goods in East Africa. Most of the companies ignored these instructions. The Zambian government decided to force them to comply by executive and legislative instruments prohibiting the importation of various goods from Rhodesia. By 1967 Zambia had managed to reduce its imports from Rhodesia to 11 percent of its total imports and by 1969 to 7 percent.

There are critics who hammer on President Kaunda's decision in 1971 to import two million bags of corn from Rhodesia to save the Zambian population from starving. Unfortunate as the decision might have been, it should not keep the world from recognizing that no other state suffered as much as Zambia in the enforcement of economic sanctions against Rhodesia. Few leaders in the world would have made the decision in the first place to apply economic sanctions against

Rhodesia if they had been in President Kaunda's position. Malawi and Botswana have not strictly enforced economic sanctions against Rhodesia for fear of retaliation.

The Proposed "Settlements"

UDI was effected to halt any advance towards majority rule in Rhodesia. Smith pledged to resist any settlement with Britain that would guarantee African rule in Rhodesia in the "foreseeable future." One year after UDI, British Prime Minister Harold Wilson attempted to lure the Smith regime into a settlement of the Rhodesian crisis. Wilson and Smith met on the British ship *Tiger* in December 1966 and drew up the Tiger Settlement.[27] This proposed to establish a Legislative Assembly of sixty-seven seats of which thirty-three were to be called "A" roll seats, seventeen "B" roll seats, and seventeen were to be reserved exclusively for Europeans. The "A" roll seats would be elected by voters with higher income, property, and educational qualifications. Such an arrangement would have assured that the candidates for the thirty-three "A" roll seats would be voted for by a predominantly white electorate and the candidates for the seventeen "B" roll seats by a predominantly African electorate. Since the other seventeen seats were reserved for Europeans, they would have been elected by an exclusively white electorate. This settlement would have guaranteed the Europeans fifty seats and the Africans a possible seventeen. There was, in fact, no provision that would have prevented Europeans from standing for the seventeen "B" roll seats.

And yet the Smith regime rejected the Tiger Settlement. What frightened them was Paragraph 3, which extended the "B" roll franchise to include all Africans over thirty who satisfied the citizenship and residence qualifications. It also retained cross-voting for all seats.[28] What this paragraph implied, at least to the frightened minds of the Smith regime, is that, first, every African of the age of thirty or above would qualify to be a "B" roll voter. Therefore the regime was faced with a variable it could not control. Second, the cross-voting would allow the "B" roll voters to vote for the candidates for the thirty-three "A" roll seats, although four "B" roll votes would be equivalent to only one "A" roll vote. ("A" roll voters were also to be allowed to vote for the candidates for the seventeen "B" roll seats, and four "A" roll votes were to count as one "B" vote.) The regime believed that such an arrangement favored the Africans. Although two-thirds of the African population in Rhodesia is less than the age of thirty, the third which is thirty years old or more represents about 1,800,000 Africans. According to the proposed Tiger Settlement, these Africans would have qualified for the "B" roll franchise and in voting for the candidates to fill the thirty-three "A" roll seats would have counted as 450,000 "A" roll votes. There are only 220,000 Europeans in Rhodesia, and of these not more than 100,000 fulfill the age, citizenship, residential, income, property, and educational qualifications to be voters. It seemed as if the Africans of Zimbabwe could attain control of the government under the Tiger Proposals.

However, under these proposals the Africans never would have attained control of the government because of Paragraph 2, which distributed the seats in the House of Assembly in favor of the Europeans. This paragraph specifically allotted seventeen seats to the Europeans without specifically allotting any seat to the Africans in the Legislative Assembly.

But the Smith regime rejected the Tiger Proposals because the very thought that African majority rule was theoretically possible scared them.

In October 1968 the British Prime Minister tried again to arrive at some settlement with the Rhodesians. Wilson and Smith met again on the British ship *Fearless* off the coast of Gibraltar, where they had previously met on the *Tiger*. Britain came out with the Fearless Proposals.[30] The Smith regime rejected these too because they contained variables which the regime could not control. The regime did not want any settlement that even remotely opened a way to majority rule in Rhodesia.

To the surprise of the world, on November 25, 1971 the British government and the Smith regime arrived at an agreement.[31] The Smith regime had rejected the *Tiger* and *Fearless* documents mainly because of the requirement to give Africans over the age of thirty a vote. The regime accepted what came to be known as the Home-Smith Agreement, partly because this requirement was restricted.[32] The Agreement begins by agreeing that "the Constitution of Rhodesia will be the Constitution adopted in Rhodesia in 1969 modified . . . "[33] The 1969 Rhodesian Constitution confirmed Rhodesia's independence under the white minority government of Smith.

The Smith regime accepted the British modifications to the 1969 Constitution because the regime could easily control the education and income requirements and thus deny the Africans their voting power if it became threatening. For as we saw in Chapter 1, although the new constitution theoretically assured Africans additional seats in the House of Assembly as more of them became enfranchised, their franchise would still depend on their (government-controlled) income and education.

Smith thought the settlement would be acceptable to both whites and blacks in Rhodesia. But he had shockingly misunderstood the African. He said on the BBC in November 1971 that "the African in Rhodesia is the happiest African in Africa. He is not interested in politics." A few months afterwards that African who was supposed to be uninterested in politics rejected the settlement on which Smith had placed all of his hopes.

Response From the White World

Although UDI was effected for the purpose of maintaining white supremacy in Rhodesia, Rhodesia has become an embarrassment to the white world. The principles of democracy, which the Western world claims are the standard of "civilized" government, are openly flouted in Rhodesia. Condemnation of the Rhodesian system of government has been voiced from all corners of the white world. But one thing must be made clear: The verbal condemnation of UDI should not be taken to mean that the white world would like to see the black man rule Rhodesia. It would be satisfied if the Rhodesian whites would only behave like "civilized" people are supposed to behave. In other words, the white world would be happy if the Rhodesians were to grant the African people more freedom of speech, more freedom of movement, and a little more education; the whites would of course retain the reins of power.

When Rhodesia effected its UDI the United States delegate in the Security Council said, "A small, stubborn and sadly mistaken minority has seized sole power in a effort to dominate the lives of the vast and unwilling majority of the population of Southenn Rhodesia. . . . "[34] Chief delegate De Beus of the Netherlands concurred: "The unlawful declaration of independence in Southern Rhodesia undoubtedly constitutes one of the most serious situations the Security Council has ever faced."[35]

But when the states which were disgusted by Rhodesia's UDI were called upon to support a draft resolution in the Security council for effective and vigorous action against Rhodesia, they balked. The Netherlands assisted Rhodesia in evading the effects of the sanctions. Dutch ships, the *Tjibodas*, the *Tjipandok*, and the *Zuiderkerk*; and German ships, the *Tugelaland*, the *Krugerland*, and the *Palabera* transported Rhodesian goods to ports all over the world. Rhodesian goods were smuggled through the Dutch ports of Amsterdam, Rotterdam, and Antwerp. Italian companies like Ferocimetal of Milan and Swiss companies like Nitrex and Hendelsgesellschaft bought Rhodesian goods and sold European goods to Rhodesia in defiance of Security Council sanction resolutions.[36] American companies like Union Carbide, the

Vanadium Corporation of America, and the American Potash and Chemical Corporation continued pouring investments in Rhodesia in violation of the sanction resolutions.[37] The United States Congress authorized American companies to buy Rhodesian chrome in violation of the sanction resolutions.[38]

Why did these "great democracies" that had condemned UDI and the oppressiveness of the Rhodesian political system violate the sanction resolutions of the United Nations? The answer is clear. Condemning UDI is one thing; participating in the overthrow of a white government to be replaced by an African government is another. The Western states are not prepared to throw one of their own to the dogs. Since economic sanctions were directed towards overthrowing the Rhodesian government, the Western world was not prepared to take active part. And yet these same governments had to appear to be supporting the sanction measures.

The irony of the Rhodesian crisis is that even the white socialist governments were not prepared to take part in any scheme directed towards overthrowing the white Rhodesian regime. When UDI was effected, the socialist states in the Security Council were not interested in discussing what should be done to suppress the illegal regime of Rhodesia. Instead they saw in the Rhodesian crisis an opportunity to attack their traditional enemies, the United States and Britain, and to subject to scrutiny what they regarded as "the social and political nature and essence of Anglo-American relations."[39] Nowhere in the records of the Security Council or the General Assembly do the socialist states suggest ways of dealing with the Rhodesian crisis. In December 1966 the Soviet Union and Bulgaria abstained when Security Council Resolution 232 (1966), which first designated the situation in Rhodesia as "a threat to international peace and security," was adopted. While they claimed that the resolution was too weak, they did not suggest what should be done in the light of British refusal to take effective independent action against Rhodesia. Even when they later voted in 1968 for Security

Council Resolution 253, imposing comprehensive sanctions on Rhodesia, they did not do so in the hope of overthrowing the Rhodesian regime. They voted for the resolution to appease the Afro-Asian states.[40]

Yugoslavia permitted the Italian ship *Hierax* to sail from the Yugoslav port of Split with Rhodesian ferro-chrome. Polish authorities, after allowing the Cypriot ship *Goodwill* to unload Rhodesian tobacco at the Polish port of Szczecin, allowed the tobacco to be transported to West Germany by barge after the tobacco had been on Polish soil for sixteen days.[41] The socialist states were not eager to support economic sanctions against Rhodesia. They made noise in the chambers of the Security Council, but an examination of the record shows that their contribution towards ending the Rhodesian crisis was nil.

Such were the responses of the white world towards the Rhodesian crisis: Neither the capitalist states nor the socialist states were willing to take effective action to terminate white supremacy in Rhodesia. Could it be that the common denominator among the socialist states, the capitalist Western states, and the Rhodesian rebel regime is the color of the skin of those who control political power in these states? If this is true then the Africans of Rhodesia must be warned of the white world conspiracy that will perpetuate white supremacy in Rhodesia.

NOTES

1. "Britain's Problem Child—Southern Rhodesia," *Central African Examiner*, November 1963.

2. See "Deepening Divisions," *Central African Examiner*, June 1963.

3. "Southern Rhodesia Double Deals," *Central African Examiner*, October 1964.

4. "Sir Roy to lead New Rhodesia Party," *East Africa and Rhodesia*, August 20, 1964.

5. *Ibid.*

6. Larry Bowman, *Trends in Rhodesian Politics with Special Reference to African Advancement and the Independence Issue*, Paper presented to the East African Institute of Social Research, January 1966.

7. A. Skeen, *Prelude to Independence: Skeen's 115 Days* (Capetown: Nasionale Boekhandel, 1966), p. 52.

8. "Prison Undergraduates," *Central African Examiner*, April 1964.

9. "Final Decision Soon," *Sunday Mail*. October 10, 1964.

10. *Sunday Mail*, October 31, 1965.

11. *Ibid.*

12. See Appendix

13. Leonard T. Kapungu, *The United Nations and Economic Sanctions Against Rhodesia* (Lexington, Massachusetts: D. C. Heath, 1973). See also Leonard T. Kapungu, "Economic Sanctions in the Rhodesian Context," in Yassin El Ayoutyand Hugh Brooks, *Africa and International Organizations* (The Hague: Nijhoff, 1973).

14. U.N. Document, Security Council Resolution, 232 (1966).

15. U.N. Document, Security Council Resolution, 253 (1968).

16. O.A.U. Document, AHG/18 (III).

17. Julius Nyerere, *Freedom and Socialism/Uhuru na Ujamaa* (Dar es Salaam: Oxford University Press, 1968), p. 128.

18. Roy Welensky, *4000 Days* (London: Collins, 1964).

19. U.N. Document S/7781/Add 1.

20. See W.J. Levy, Inc., *The Economics and Logistics of an Embargo on Oil and Petroleum Products from Rhodesia*, Report Prepared for the United Nations Security-General, February 1966.

21. U.N. Document S/7781/Add 1.

22. U.N. Document S/7781/Add 2.

23. U.N. Document S/9252/Add 1/Annex 1.

24. Britain provided Rhodesia with $88,112,000 worth of goods in 1965 or about 29 percent of Rhodesia's total imports.

25. *Times* (London), September 5, 1964.

26. U.N. Document S/9252/Add 1.

27. *Rhodesia, Proposals for a Settlement, 1966*, London, HMSO, CMND 3159.

28. *Ibid.*, p. 9.

29. *Ibid.*

30. See *Rhodesia, Proposals for a Settlement, 1968*, London, HMSO.

31. *Rhodesia, Proposals for a Settlement, 1971*, London, CMND 4835.

32. British Foreign Secretary Sir Alec Douglas-Home negotiated the Agreement with Ian Smith.

33. *Proposals for a Settlement, 1971.*

34. U.N. Document S/PV1254, p. 17.

35. U.N. Document S/PV1260, p. 19.

36. See U.N. Document S/9252/Add 1, Annex XI, S/9844/Add 2, Annex VII, pp.97–100. For an analysis see Kapungu, *United Nations and Economic Sanctions.*

37. *Foreign Economic Interests and Decolonization* (United Nations, New York, 1969).

38. See *Washington Post*, November 4, 1971.

39. U.N. Document S/PV1259, p. 30.

40. U.N. Document S/PV1428, p. 22.

41. U.N. Document S/9252/Add 1, Annex XI, pp. 20–23. For details of the evasion of sanctions see Kapungu, *United Nations and Economic Sanctions.*

CHAPTER 4

The Dilemma of the Churches in Rhodesia

African Religion

The Zimbabwean people are very religious. Since long before any white person set foot in Rhodesia, they have had religious practices centered on two beliefs. The first is that there is a Supreme Being called "Mwari," at times also called "the Man on the Mountain." This Supreme Being is believed to be the creator of the universe and the father of mankind, capable of controlling the destiny of all creatures, human and non-human, of delivering blessings to the good, and of punishing the wicked. It is believed that this Supreme Being has given laws to enable man to distinguish the good from the wicked. Traditional religion also holds that a curse would fall on anyone who swore in vain using the Supreme Being's name, on anyone who disrespects his elders, steals, murders, covets another man's wife, or commits adultery. Whoever commits any of these wicked acts is required to repent publicly or else the Supreme Being will punish him and his posterity. For example, the son who hits his mother is required, as a sign of penance, to dress in rags, smear his body with ashes, and go from village to village asking for forgiveness. Until the law proscribed it, a man who stole had his hands put on hot bricks, and a man who committed adultery had his head covered with a crown of thorns.

The second belief on which the religious practices of the Zimbabweans are based is the immortality of the soul. The African believes that a man does not die; death is simply a transformation from one state of life to another. Even after the body has ceased to function the spirit continues. A good man is more powerful in death than in life; a wicked man is more wicked in death than in life. Each spirit continues to affect the lives of his family, his relatives, and friends.

These two beliefs are brought into harmony with each other through a system of communication. The Supreme Being is considered so powerful that no living human being would communicate directly with Him. A person has to ask his spirits, his dead ancestors, to intercede for him with the Supreme Being. Thus, one has to be on good terms with the spirits so that they may always intercede for him. There are ceremonies like *mashave*, *Kuteura mudzimu*, and *Kurowa guva* which must be performed by every African in order to remain in the love of the spirits and the Supreme Being; the majority of Zimbabweans today still perform these ceremonies.

The Coming of White Churches

In the sixteenth and seventeenth centuries Christian missionaries began coming to Zimbabwe from Europe. The first arrivals were Catholic Jesuits. With the coming of white settlers in the 1890's, other mission churches poured into Rhodesia—Anglicans, British Methodists, American Methodists, the Salvation Army, and the Dutch Reformed Church. While the settlers saw the Africans as barbarians, the missionaries considered them pagans and worshippers of false gods.

It would have been easy for the churches to convert the

TABLE 2

AFRICAN EDUCATION UNDER MISSIONARIES
(1901–1960)

YEAR	NUMBER OF PUPILS	NUMBER OF SCHOOLS
1901	265	3
1910	9,873	115
1920	43,091	750
1930	107,122	1,422
1940	111,686	1,392
1950	232,689	2,232
1960	448,891	2,727

Source: Thomas M. Franck, *Race and Nationalism: The Struggle for Power in Rhodesia-Nyasaland* (New York: Fordham University Press, 1960), p. 118, and *Annual Report by the Director of Native Education*, 1961, CR10, Salisbury, 1962.

Africans to Christianity had they only treated them as people with a developed culture. The Supreme Being of the African is the God of the white man; the spirits of the African are the saints of the white man. Such comparisons the white man refused to accept, for he wanted to believe that he was bringing something new to the African. He "taught" him the Ten Commandments as if the African had no similar ethical precepts of his own.

Not only did the white men refuse to accept these similarities, they involved themselves in contradictions. While they called the African communication with the spirits sinful, they taught the African to pray to Saint Ignatius, Saint Catherine, and others. The Africans did not even know these white people, so they could not verify whether they had lived the good life. But they were taught to pray to them and forget their spirits. While the Africans were told that to perform ceremonies on the graves of their dead was sinful, every Rhodes and Founder's Day the missionary teachers joined the white settlers in processions to the statues of Rhodes and adorned his statues and his grave with garlands of flowers. The Africans were expected to forget their dead while the white people continued to remember theirs.

Missionary Education

It is indisputable that the white missionaries brought formal education to the African of Rhodesia. Without missionary schools most Africans would be illiterate, and this African would not be writing this book. The governments of Rhodesia were simply not interested in building schools for the African. But the missionaries competed with each other in building schools for Africans, so eager were they to convert the African to the Christianity of their denomination. African education in missionary hands expanded from year to year as shown in Table 2.

By the time the Rhodesian Front came to power in December 1962, the total enrollment of Africans in mission schools was as show in Tables 3 and 4. Considering the reluctance of the Rhodesian governments to finance African education, the above figures indicate not a small contribution from the churches.

The irony of the missionary activity in Rhodesia is that the Africans who go through missionary schools are the bitterest critics of the churches. Most of the Africans who have attained Grade 12 in missionary schools never go to church after leaving school except for weddings and funerals. There are several reasons for this. First, the missionaries insist that an African who attends their schools belong to their denomination. Thus, when an African boy goes to a Catholic school for Grades 1 to

TABLE 3

AFRICAN PRIMARY SCHOOL ENROLLMENT IN MISSION SCHOOLS

ENROLLMENT	BOYS	GIRLS
Sub-Std A (Grade 1)	56,264	49,556
Sub-Std B(Grade 2)	50,973	43,039
Std 1 (Grade 3)	46,547	39,406
Std 2 (Grade 4)	38,863	31,015
Std 3 (Grade 5)	34,631	23,830
Std 4 (Grade 6)	11,854	7,054
Std 5 (Grade 7)	9,267	4,628
Std 6 (Grade 8)	7,669	3,551
Total	256,068	202,079

Source: *Annual Report by the Director of Native Education, 1961*, CR10, Salisbury, 1962, p. 12

TABLE 4

AFRICAN SECONDARY SCHOOL ENROLLMENT IN MISSION SCHOOLS

ENROLLMENT	BOYS	GIRLS
Form I (Grade 9)	1,327	390
Form II (Grade 10)	919	253
Form III (Grade 11)	278	40
Form IV (Grade 12)	235	21
Total	2,759	704

Source: *Annual Report by the Director of Native Education*, 1961, CR10, Salisbury, 1962, p. 12

6 he must be baptized in the Catholic church. He may go to an Anglican school for Grades 7 to 10 and must be "baptized" again in the Anglican church. If he goes to a Methodist school for Grades 11 and 12 he must be "baptized" in the Methodist church. By the time he finishes Grade 12 he has been a Catholic, an Anglican, and a Methodist; in the end he is none of these. Other members of his family may go to school with different sects and may also end up by belonging to none of them. The African wonders whether there is a God for every denomination. He finds that he became a Catholic, an Anglican, and a Methodist not by conviction but for expediency —to get an education. When he finishes his education he does not have the conviction of a Christian and the church has no longer any function in his life.

Secondly, while the African is at the mission school he comes into contact with the white man's behavior and concludes that the missionary is no different from any other white man. For example, at the Anglican Mission of Saint Augustine, there are two communities of Sisters, one for the white Sisters and the other for the African Sisters. The white Sisters' group is called the Order of the Holy Paraclete and that of the African Sisters is the "Chita Che Zita Rinoyera," which is simply a translation of Holy Paraclete. The Sisters are dressed differently—the white Sisters in beautiful, immaculate robes and the African Sisters in very cheap, shabby ones. African Sisters have their own quarters, and the white Sisters have well-furnished, more beautiful quarters. Worse still, the white Sisters and the white Fathers would send their clothes, including their underwear, for the African Sisters to wash by hand and to iron. The African student watches this and he remembers it.

Let us also take a Catholic example. An African student goes to Kutama Catholic Secondary School. During the holidays he goes to live with his parents in the Salisbury African Police Training School, where his father is a policeman. He has been taught at Kutama Mission to go to church every day. During the holidays he decides to follow the habit, but there are no Catholic church services in the police depot during the week. He decides to go to the Catholic cathedral only three miles away. He and his girl friend are immaculately dressed. They ride their bicycles to the cathedral and enter the main hall. They kneel down and as they are deep in prayer a white hand pats the boy's shoulder and a voice says, "No Africans are allowed in the main hall; follow me." In obedience, he and his girl friend follow the white man into the sacristy and they are told to attend Mass from there. They can see the officiating priest through small spaces in the wall of the sacristy—but only when he is on the right side of the altar. Communion time arrives. The white man who had led them away from the main hall reappears and tells them that Africans are not allowed to receive Holy Communion at the altar rail. The boy and his girl friend receive Communion in the sacristy and depart. The scene recurs every day of his holidays and is repeated holiday after holiday. The boy has been taught that Holy Communion is the living body of Christ, the Son of God. But the humiliation accumulates, and the boy concludes that the churches are a fake, a means to sustain white supremacy in Rhodesia and humiliate the African.

The African student has seen the missionary at work. He has grown to realize that the missionary is part and parcel of the oppressive system of Rhodesia. He asks himself whether the good the missionary does outweighs the evil the missionary supports. If his answer is positive he cannot effectively challenge the system of Rhodesia. Most young men and women who have passed through missionary hands have come out with a negative answer to this question. Bitterness outweighs gratitude, and the missionaries have seen the very people they educated turning against them.

Churches and Position of Influence

Through schools and places of worship, the missionaries in Rhodesia are in touch with a large section of African population. Therefore, the position of the churches as a source of influence among the Africans is of no small significance. For example, the total Catholic community of Rhodesia in 1971 was 335,000 communicants, of whom only 27,246 were white; the total British Methodist community of Rhodesia was 112,500, of whom only 2,344 were white.[1] The rest were Africans. But despite the fact that Africans form the majority of the Christian community, it was not until 1965 that the American Methodist Church appointed an African as bishop, and it was not until the closing months of 1972 that the Catholic and Anglican Churches appointed Africans as bishops. Yet both the Catholic and Anglican Churches had their first African priests more than twenty-five years ago. There is no law in Rhodesia which forbids the churches to appoint African clergymen to positions of authority. The only reason the churches in Rhodesia did not appoint Africans to these positions is that the missionaries are not different from the other white Rhodesians. Like them, the missionaries think the Africans are incapable of running their own affairs, and that white people must shape African destinies. If there are few African bishops in Rhodesia because there are not many African clergymen to choose from, it must be asked why the churches have failed to recruit these clergymen.

Furthermore, the churches in Rhodesia are aware of their position of influence among the Africans. What would happen if this position of influence is controlled by an African? Bishop Abel Muzorewa of the American Methodist Church has demonstrated how an African bishop can effectively be a force of political mobilization among the Africans against the oppressive Rhodesian system. Bishop Muzorewa believes that as a Christian he cannot tolerate evil and that it is the duty of Christians to challenge evil in whatever form it takes. He further believes that as a bishop, the spiritual head of his church in Rhodesia, he must lead his followers against the evils of the Rhodesian system. In 1966, barely a year after he had been made a bishop, he declared that Rhodesia's UDI was an attempt to sustain an evil political system. He called upon his fellow Christians to speak out against it. In June 1970, when he addressed a special annual conference of his church, Bishop Muzorewa candidly told the assembled delegates, "I will fight as a Christian against the Rhodesian political system."[2] The Rhodesian government did not look with favor on this man of God who could identify evil and fight against it. Realizing how influential an African bishop can be among Africans who have always been taught to do as the bishop or priest bids, on September 2, 1970 the Rhodesian government banned Bishop Muzorewa from the tribal trust lands in which most of the Africans live. According to the United Methodist Church, "This meant that he could not visit 75 percent of his churches."[3]

But the Bishop continued the struggle. In November 1971 British Foreign Secretary Sir Alec Douglas-Home and Rhodesian rebel leader Ian Smith agreed on a settlement of the Rhodesian crisis and decided to send a British commission to Rhodesia to determine whether the settlement was acceptable to the people of Rhodesia "as a whole." After studying the settlement proposals Bishop Muzorewa was "convinced beyond doubt that acceptance of these proposals by Africans would be a betrayal of the Africans, dead and living and yet to be born." He declared, "We cannot be vendors of our own heritage and rights."[4] He called all the African people of Rhodesia to forget their petty differences and unite for a higher common objective. The Bishop and other dedicated Zimbabweans formed the African National Council to campaign against the settlement proposal. At a press conference the Bishop declared,

> I wish at this point to call upon all the African people—sons and daughters of the soil—at home and abroad, poor and rich, educated or uneducated, young and old, to stop now quarreling, bickering, and end the division which continues to cripple our struggle for freedom . . . . We are all condemned as *Black People.*[5]

In an unprecedented show of unity the African people of Zimbabwe heeded the call of the bishop and rejected the proposals.

Churches and UDI

The Rhodesian Churches did not protest against the government's racist policies until the Rhodesian Front was elected to power in December 1962. Then it dawned on them that under the ruthless RF government even the churches might have to suffer. Only then did they become aware of the injustices of the Rhodesian society, and only then did they swing their support to the demands of justice.

After the RF came to power, Bishop K. Skelton of the Anglican Church, Bishop Ralph E. Dodge of the United Methodist Church, and Bishop Donal R. Lamont of the Catholic Church began to speak out against the evils of Rhodesian society. In 1964 Bishop Dodge said in a radio interview that "Rhodesia was guilty of practicing racialism, segregation, and apartheid."[6] The Rhodesian government considered this a bad example from a leader of the church. Bishop Dodge was declared an "undesirable alien" and was deported. The United Methodist Church had now tasted the salt and began vigorously to condemn the evils of the Rhodesian society. In May 1964 the Rhodesian Methodist Church called on the British government to suspend the 1961 Constitution and call for a constitutional conference to (1) adjust the Land Apportionment Act, (2) revise the franchise, (3) increase African representation in Parliament.[7]

A few months before UDI the Protestant churches of Rhodesia held a consultation on "The Church and Human Relations." Ninety members, representing all of the Protestant churches, issued a report calling for social, educational, and political reforms. They condemned the Land Apportionment Act and the 1961 Constitution.[8] In October 1965 the British Council of Churches and the Archbishop of Canter-

bury, Dr. Michael Ramsey, called for British military force
against Rhodesia in the event of UDI. The Archbishop declared, "If our Government thought it practicable and desira-
ble to use force in discharging not a new, but a continuing
obligation to Rhodesia, then as Christian people, unless we are
pacifists, it would be right to say that force should be used."[9]
Now the churches accepted what the Africans had been saying all along, that the Rhodesian regime can be brought to its
senses only if force is used.

When Ian Smith effected his UDI on November 11, 1965,
the Rhodesian churches unanimously condemned it as an act
of rebellion that contradicted Christian teachings. The Christian Council of Churches of Rhodesia issued its statement on
November 26, 1965:

> In humble submission to the sovereignty of Almighty God and
> the judgement of our Lord Jesus Christ, we affirm our present
> loyalty to Her Majesty the Queen within the Constitution
> which is at present the Constitution accepted by the lawful
> Parliament of Rhodesia 1961.
>
> We affirm our present loyalty to His Excellency the Gover-
> nor of Rhodesia as the Queen's lawful governor according to
> the Constitution.
>
> We repudiate misuse of the Queen's name in Constitutional
> matters, the Queen having the clear duty as a constitutional
> monarch to reject any advice, whether from her Prime Minis-
> ter in Britain or from her Prime Minister in Rhodesia, which is
> contrary to the Constitution itself, affirmed by the British and
> Rhodesian Parliaments.
>
> We judge the proclamation of a new constitution of
> Rhodesia by a group of Ministers, without the assent of the
> Parliament or the Crown, to be an unlawful act and any
> further enactments of Parliament to be unlawful unless con-
> firmed by the lawful Governor.
>
> We regret the great blow delivered by this act to the concept
> of constitutional law brought to Africa by a Western civiliza-
> tion nurtured in Christianity.
>
> We note the intimidation of both black and white is increas-
> ing in many insidious ways. As a result, more people than ever
> are now afraid to exercise their right of freedom of speech.

We are deeply concerned that information is frequently suppressed. A particularly serious instance of this is the means by which people are taken away from their homes, while it is an offence for friends or relatives to make known their whereabouts.

We look forward earnestly to and pledge ourselves to work for the rapid restoration of constitutional government in our land.

We affirm the right and duty of Christians to witness publicly and privately in this situation to the truth as they believe it to be, clearly, wisely, charitably, and according to their opportunities.

But witness alone is not enough. The present situation has been the culmination not principally of constitutional or political dispute but of racial division and a lack of good faith. If this continues the graver and deeper will be the wounds in the body of mankind, and in Christ's Body the Church, here in Rhodesia and far beyond.

We believe that the Church, ministers and laymen together, should turn at once to its renewal at the fount of the healing of Christ, and be untiring in its own forgiving, reconciling and healing work in His name.[10]

The Roman Catholic Bishops of Rhodesia issued their statement on November 28, 1965, in a Pastoral Message. They said:

We have pointed out to you before the command of our divine Lord to imitate his own example of love, yet few have had the faith and the courage to face up to the challenge. Here let us say it again: According to our Christian faith, all principles of division, all national and cultural particularities, all social, political and religious differentiations, are meant to be subordinated to the overall unity achieved by Christ. You are all children of God by faith in Christ Jesus . . . . There is neither Jew nor Greek, there is neither bond nor free, there is neither male nor female. For you are all one in Christ Jesus (Gal. 3:26–8). Whosoever, therefore, deliberately despises this disposition of God for his human creatures is guilty of a grave act of dishonor to the Almighty and must be considred to sin grievously.

How can we possibly profess to be followers of Christ if we do not try to respect one another and care for one another? Our

Lord's words are quite unmistakable on this point. They are both a warning and a programme of action: "By this shall all men know that you are my disciples, if you love one another" (John 13:35). He even goes further; he identifies himself with our fellowmen.

And God knows there is plenty of opportunity about us for exercising practical charity here in Rhodesia . . . . Look at the unequitable distribution of land in this country; the scandal of those working conditions in which normal family life is made impossible; the often inadequate wages paid to servants, the humiliation of discriminatory legislation, the inequalities of opportunity in education. Examine these things and judge if we can ever be a united and happy people while they remain. We hear much about our rights these days, but little about our responsibilities as a supposedly Christian people.[11]

The churches of Rhodesia had finally spoken, tabulating the ills of Rhodesian society which they had refrained from condemning for more than seventy-five years. But they had become witnesses to the truth of the statement of Edmund Burke, "For Evil to triumph it is enough that good men do nothing." In 1965 evil triumphed in Rhodesia.

Churches and the Land Tenure Act

The Churches did not begin to criticize the Rhodesian political system until their own interests were at stake. They had never protested the establishment of two voters' rolls, one for the Europeans and another for the Africans. In fact they supported the 1961 Constitution which had two rolls. The difference between the 1961 Constitution and the 1969 Constitution, which the churches criticized, was that the 1961 Constitution called the predominantly European voters' roll the "A" roll and the predominantly African voters' roll the "B" roll. In 1969 the "A" roll was called the European roll and the "B" roll was called the African roll. To the churches the 1969 Constitution was discriminatory while the 1961 Constitution was not, although the effects were the same.

But what infuriated the churches most was the Land Tenure Act which was associated with the 1969 Constitution. Since 1930 the churches had not protested the Land Apportionment Act, which divided land between the races. In 1969 the Rhodesian rebel government enacted the Land Tenure Act, which came into operation on the date the 1969 Constitution came into effect. There is little difference between the Land Apportionment Act of 1930 and the Land Tenure Act of 1969, but that little difference is what affected the churches of Rhodesia and produced their outcry against the Rhodesian political system. The Land Apportionment Act was vague regarding the separation of races in educational institutions, hospitals, and boarding houses, although for years the interpretation of the Act was that people had to be separated according to race in these places. The churches had usually followed this interpretation. For example, at the Anglican mission of Saint Augustine there were African Sisters' quarters and white Sisters' quarters, as noted above; they were, however, on the same piece of land. At Chishawasha Catholic Mission there were African Sisters' quarters and white Sisters' quarters, again on the same piece of land. There were white churches and African churches, white schools and African schools all over Rhodesia. Now and again a white church school would enroll one or two African students, as the Catholic School of Saint George in Salisbury did in the 1960's. The government would complain, but by and large the churches were allowed this limited discretion in their interpretation of the Land Apportionment Act. Thus they refrained from attacking the Act under which the African population languished.

The 1969 Constitution and the Land Tenure Act (1969) cancelled the discretion the churches had under the Land Apportionment Act. Section 3 of the Land Tenure Act was a bombshell:

> 1. The Minister may prescribe that attendance for a specified purpose at a specified place or premises or class of places or premises to which members of the pub-

lic are admitted shall constitute occupation for the purposes of this Act, and any person who attends for such purpose at such place or premises or class of places or premises shall be regarded for the purposes of this Act as occupying the land concerned.

2. A person who:
   (a) attends at a school or other educational institution as a teacher or pupil thereat; or
   (b) attends at a clinic, hospital or other medical institution as a doctor other employee thereat or as a patient; or
   (c) stays at a hotel, motel, boarding house, club at which residential facilities are provided or other such premises;

   shall be regarded for the purposes of this Act as occupying the land on which the educational institution, medical institution, hotel, motel, boarding house, club or other such premises as the case may be, is situated.[12]

The Act proceeded to demarcate lands as European or African almost on the same pattern as the Land Apportionment Act. Europeans were given 44,952,900 acres while the Africans were given 44,944,500 acres; national reserves were allocated 6,617,400 acres.[13]

This Act meant that white and black clergymen could no longer live on the same land even if their quarters were segregated. Missionary schools like the Catholic school of Chishawasha or the Methodist school of Epworth could not operate under such a law since they depended on both white and black clergy staff. Mutambara, Old Umtali, and Nyadiri missions of the American Methodist Church are on white land and Mrewa and Nyamazuwe of the same Church are on African land. Strict enforcement of the Act would have forced all these African schools to close.

In a Pastoral Message the Catholic bishops of Rhodesia condemned both the Constitution and the Land Tenure Act as "in many respects completely contrary to Christian teaching."[14] In another Pastoral Message the Catholic bishops continued their attack on the Land Tenure Act. They stated:

It may well be that we shall also be denied, in violation of our conscience, the right to educate in our schools whomsoever we will. We may even be forced by segregation to refuse hospital beds to anyone not of the race approved in that area. Priests and nuns and teaching brothers may have to be segregated in their communities according to their racial origins. The whole future of the church in Rhodesia is thus at stake.[15]

The Catholic bishops went on to threaten to close all schools and hospitals under their control if the Act was not revised.

Seventeen heads of churches and Christian organizations in Rhodesia met in June 1969 to coordinate their attacks on the Land Tenure Act and the 1969 Constitution. They declared:

There is a great deal in the *Bible* that bears directly on the problems of race. The proclamation of the Gospel creates a multiracial community "from every nation, from all tribes and peoples and tongues." The tensions of creating such a community are reflected in the New Testament writings, but Christians believe that in Christ God has broken down the walls of division between man and man. All human differences of race or tribe or nation lose their divisive significance through the reconciling work of Christ.[16]

Of the seventeen who signed this message four were Africans: Bishop A.T. Muzorewa of the United Methodist Church, Reverend H.H. Kachidza of the Bible Societies in Rhodesia, Reverend A.M. Ndhlela of the Methodist Church, and Reverend E.T.J. Nemapare of the African Methodist Church. The rest were whites, and that was what eventually compromised the value of the message. Ian Smith was confident that if he negotiated with the white leaders of the churches they would see "sense and reason" and compromise with him. And indeed the white church leaders did negotiate with Smith and reached a white man's understanding.

The understanding was that the Land Tenure Act would go into effect, but the government either would not insist on immediate enforcement of certain provisions of the Act or would give the churches special licenses to exempt them from these provisions. The white leaders agreed, although they admitted that this agreement "left possible implementation [of the whole Act] as an ax to hold over the head of the church."[17]

Once again the white church leaders demonstrated that there is a point beyond which no white man in Rhodesia will go in supporting a black man's struggle. The interests of the churches were satisfied by Smith. They relented despite the fact that the African still suffered untold hardships under those provisions of the Act which were implemented.

Churches and the Anglo-Rhodesian Proposed Settlement

In November 1971 British Foreign Minister Sir Alec Douglas-Home and Rhodesian Prime Minister Ian Smith agreed that a British commission be sent to Rhodesia to determine the opinion of the people of Rhodesia "as a whole" on the Anglo-Rhodesian Proposed Settlement, which in effect was to legalize the Rhodesian rebellion of 1965 and leave the government of Rhodesia in the hands of the whites.

Britain has always recognized the churches of Rhodesia as a responsible body of opinion, and the Pearce Commission, which was assigned the task of testing the opinion of the Rhodesians, went to Rhodesia intending to give more weight to what church leaders would say than to the views of the black political parties—the African nationalists.[18] But church opinion was divided, although the majority of the church leaders were against the settlement. The Christian Council of Rhodesia, which represents nearly all the churches, voted on the settlement. Twenty-five representatives voted against the settlement and nine voted for it. Those who voted against it did so on the grounds that it was "unjust and un-humanitarian." Those who voted for it, led by Anglican Bishop Paul Burrough of Mashonaland, believed "that the agreement is the best that blacks can hope to get now."[19]

It is gratifying to the Africans that the majority of the

church leaders came out against the proposed Anglo-Rhodesian settlement. The Pearce Commission could not ignore their views. As Stanley Meisler of the *Los Angeles Times* noted, "The Commission can dismiss black nationalists as militant hotheads representing a minority. But it can hardly do the same with church leaders, most of whom are white and highly respected in Britian."[30] What makes the Africans uneasy with the church leaders, however, is their ability to compromise and to see what Ian Smith calls "sense and reason." Because most of them are white, they can easily be lured into trusting the word of a fellow white man. The Roman Catholic bishops had also come out against the settlement, but what Father R. H. Randolph, the Communications Secretary of the Catholic bishops, is reported to have said did not give the Africans much confidence that church leaders would remain resolutely against the proposed settlement. Father Randolph, hitherto an impeccable critic of the Smith regime, is reported to have written that "he personally believed the agreement could become a satisfactory solution to the present deadlock in view of the fact that the alternative . . . would be a continuation of the status quo, including sanctions."[21] Father Randolph had, to use Smith's words, seen "sense and reason." It is this ability of the white man in Rhodesia to see "sense and reason" in Smith that makes Africans question the support they have so far received from the church leaders.

Churches and the Use of Violence

A society in which people are detained without trial, husbands are separated from their wives, fathers are removed from their children without explanations, people are denied jobs and means of living because of the color of their skins, unarmed demonstrators are killed and wounded—that society is violent. Such is the Rhodesian society whose political system has dehumanized the African and whose rulers have demonstratively shown that they have no conscience. How can political change be attained in such a society?

The question of whether violence should be used to induce political change has to be faced. Represented by the Zimbabwe African People's Union (ZAPU) and the Zimbabwe African National Union (ZANU), the Africans of Zimbabwe in 1966 decided in favor of using violence against the Rhodesian political system. They launched guerrilla warfare against the regime. What position have the churches taken on the issue of violence to attain political change?

The World Council of Churches has squarely faced the question of violence. And after years of scrutinizing the problems in southern Africa it has concluded that it "does not and cannot identify itself completely with any political movement, nor pass judgement on those victims of racism who are driven to violence as the only way left to them to redress grievances and open the way for a new and more just social order."[22] This is a fair conclusion and acceptable to the African people of Zimbabwe. The Executive Committee of the World Council of Churches launched a program "to combat racism," and under the program it has granted $200,000 to nineteen organizations "representing victims of racial injustice."[23] Among these there are Zimbabwean organizations. However, the World Council of Churches has stipulated that the grants made to these organizations cannot be used for the purchase of arms. The Council has pledged to raise $300,000 as a further contribution to its battle against racism in southern Africa. The United Methodist Church of America, the National Committee of Black Churchmen of the United States, the Church of Greece, and the New Zealand Council of Churches have already made contributions to this special fund.

But voices have been raised against the involvement of churches with movements in southern Africa which use violence for political change. Dr. H. Ober Hess, the representative of the Lutheran Church in America at the meeting of the

World Council of Churches held in Ethiopia in January 1971, claimed that violence was always "antithetical" to the Christian conscience.[24] He was supported, according to press reports, by churchmen from West Germany and Britain.

The Rhodesian Christian Council supported the decision of the World Council of Churches to aid Rhodesian political movements. But "the action . . . brought sharp criticism from some of the white church leaders and brought out in the open the racial split within the Rhodesian churches."[25] Among the white church leaders who protested giving aid to Rhodesian African political movements was Anglican Bishop Paul Burrough of Mashonaland. Bishop Burrough walked out of the Anglican Consultative Council meeting in Nairobi in protest against the aid given to the nationalists.[26] Not only did Bishop Burrough seek to influence the churches not to aid the nationalists, he also sought to influence the African students at the University of Rhodesia to denounce the guerrilla activities of ZAPU and ZANU.[27] But the African students refused to listen and walked out of the service at which the Bishop was preaching. While appearing to be working in the interest of the Africans, Bishop Burrough has been very mindful of European interests in Rhodesia. Of 109,000 practising Anglicans in Rhodesia, 78,573 are whites. The Bishop caters to the interests of the white majority in his church.

The Catholic bishops are aware that the Rhodesian system breeds hatred and violence, and they confess that for a long time the churches have played a part in moderating African rage. But they are also aware that they cannot continue to succeed in distracting the Africans from using violence to redress their grievances. In their Pastoral Message on the 1969 draft Constitution and the draft Land Tenure Act the Catholic bishops noted:

> The divisive and disruptive elements contained in these proposals are not only irreconcilable with the Christian spirit of brotherhood and with the civic duty of promoting national unity, they are calculated to destroy every possibility of

achieving the common good. They offer a superficial but completely illusory hope of security for the future, and can only breed hatred and violence. If they should be implemented in a new Constitution, it will be extremely difficult for us effectively to counsel moderation to a people who have been so patient for so long under discriminatory laws and are now presented with such extreme provocation.[28]

The Constitution was implemented, and the Catholic bishops thus can no longer in good conscience "counsel moderation" to the African people.

The Conspiracy of Silence

For a long while the churches of Rhodesia have been silent in the face of an oppressive system. In fact until the Rhodesian Front came to power in 1962 the churches never thought the Rhodesian political system was oppressive; the churches were part of the system. They had an explanation for every discriminatory law passed. When the Land Apportionment Act was passed in 1930 the churches, together with the other whites, argued that the Act was to protect African lands. When the Land Husbandry Act was passed in 1951 the churches joined the other whites in arguing that the Act would prevent soil erosion in African lands. When the Unlawful Organizations Act of 1959 and the notorious Law and Order (Maintenance) Act of 1960 were passed not a single voice of protest came from the churches. When the 1961 Constitution was promulgated the churches supported it and called it a significant step of progress—despite the fact that Africans were given only token participation in the political system of their own country. The Catholic Archbishop of Salisbury, Francis W. Markall, S.J. rebuked Robert Mugabe and Leopold Takawira as Catholics to stop their campaigns against the Constitution.[29] The Archbishop urged all Catholics to vote for it.

The Catholic church in Rhodesia does not hide the fact that

throughout the years it has cooperated with the governments of Rhodesia. In a Pastoral Message of March 17, 1970, protesting the Land Tenure Act—signed by Archbishop Markall, S.J., Bishops Alysius Haene, S.M.B., of Gwelo, Adolph G. Schmitt, C.M.M., of Bulawayo, Donal R. Lamont, O. Carm., of Umtali, and Ignatius Prieto, S.M.I., of Wankie —the bishops wrote, "What has happened in this new legislation is bringing to a close the honorable and fruitful tradition of understanding and cooperation which has hitherto existed between the church and state."[30] One wonders whether the church's "honorable and fruitful tradition of understanding and cooperation" with an evil, oppressive system does not contradict what the church is supposed to stand for.

By speaking out against the post-1962 Rhodesian system the Rhodesian churches have given a misleading impression of the Rhodesian political system. They have portrayed to the world a Rhodesia that began to be unjust and oppressive after the RF came to power in 1962. In their Pastoral Message the Catholic bishops write:

> The Church is not committed to any particular form of government or to any political party. Her greatest desire is that in her mission of service and reconciliation, in pursuit of the welfare of all, she may be able to develop herself freely under any kind of government which grants recognition to the basic rights of person and family, and to the demands of the common good. This fundamental freedom is *now* endangered.[31]

Did these basic rights of person and family ever exist in Rhodesia? From the beginning of the white settlement the African was never treated as equal to the white man. Before the Rhodesia Front came to power African political movements had been banned one after another, African personal movement had been restricted, African leaders had languished in prison, and African houses were searched at night without warrant. The "fundamental freedom" the bishops talk about was not endangered for the first time in 1970; it had been endangered decades before. Where were the churches at that time? Until 1962 the churches were enforcing segregation by throwing Africans out of European churches and separating the living quarters of European and African clergymen.

The United Methodist Church implicitly confessed on November 12, 1965 that until 1962 it had not backed the people of Zimbabwe in their struggle for justice. In its *News*, the Associate General Secretary of the Board of Missions of the Methodist Church, Dr. Tracey Jones, said that "over the past four years the position of the Methodist Conference in Rhodesia has been clearly behind the aspirations of the four million Africans for their full rights in Rhodesian society."[32] But where was the United Methodist Church before the "four years" preceding 1965?

Churches and Majority Rule

Despite the criticisms that the churches have begun to level against Rhodesian society, it must be remembered that the churches of Rhodesia have always refrained from advocating the transference of political power from white hands to black. The Rhodesian Methodist Conference, for example, advocated only the increase of African participation in Parliament —not majority rule.[33]

Bishop Lamont of the Catholic church was asked on November 23, 1971, on the BBC program "Twenty-Four Hours," whether he believed in one man–one vote. The Bishop replied that he did not but rather believed that the vote should be given to those who possess "the aristocracy of the mind." The following day at a meeting of a Catholic organization of the University of London, at which I was present, Bishop Lamont was asked what he meant by the "aristocracy of the mind." The Bishop replied that he meant those capable of making sound judgements on candidates and issues. Asked how he would determine this "aristocracy of the mind," the Bishop angrily replied that he had not come to the meeting to be cross-examined.

One is struck by the similarity of the positions of Ian Smith and Bishop Lamont. Smith has said again and again that the government of Rhodesia must remain in "civilized hands." Bishop Lamont says the government must be in the hands of those who possess "the aristocracy of the mind." Smith assures that the government remains in "civilized hands" through a qualitative franchise in which property, income, and education are the measuring rods. If Bishop Lamont had to translate his "aristocracy of the mind" into practice, would he find himself taking up the measuring rods of Smith?

I do not mean to suggest that Bishop Lamont and Ian Smith hold the same position on Africans' rights. But the Bishop does show that a white clergyman in Rhodesia is conditioned to think like a white man. There is a point beyond which no white man would go in support of the black man against a fellow white man. Rhodesia provides many examples of white people who at some point in their support of the black people developed cold feet.

Churches and the Africans

It is undeniable that the churches in Rhodesia have been of great help to the African people of Zimbabwe. But for the churches to survive among the Africans both the churches and the Africans must realize each other's limitations and the facts of life that condition the behavior of each. The churches of Rhodesia are led mostly by whites. The church leaders think and react to situations like whites. They will be satisfied if more rights, but not political power, are given to the Africans.

Africans should not expect white church leaders to react like Africans. Church leaders, for their part, should not expect the Africans to be so grateful to them that they forget the inhuman conditions they live in. The Africans will distrust white church leaders just as they distrust any white person in Rhodesia. While most of the Rhodesian church leaders are fighting for equal rights for the Africans and Europeans in Rhodesia, the Africans are fighting for political power. The churches have always been far behind the aspirations of the African people. When the Africans were fighting for equal rights in the 1950's the churches were hobnobbing with the government. Only when the African consciousness developed to the level of demanding political power did the churches begin to demand what the Africans had demanded a decade before.

When the Africans come to power in Zimbabwe the churches will have to change or perish. They will be needed in a Zimbabwe nation only if they are in harmony with the spirit of the nation and the aspirations of the people. In order for them to attain such harmony their hierarchies will have to be Africanized; they should begin this now so that when the day comes they may be found ready and prepared to participate in the rebuilding of Zimbabwe.

NOTES

1. These figures were provided by the World Council of Churches.

2. See United Methodist Church, *Rhodesia 1970*, p. 3.

3. *Ibid.*

4. *African National Council Declaration*, Salisbury, January 1972.

5. *Ibid.*

6. *News*, The Methodist Church, Department of News Service, New York, November 12, 1965, p. 2.

7. Rhodesia Methodist Conference, *Statement on Rhodesia*, October 29, 1965.

8. British Council of Churches, *Rhodesia and Ourselves* (no date).

9. *Rhodesia Herald*, October 27, 1965.

10. *Rhodesia and Ourselves*, p. 20.

11. *Ibid.*

12. Rhodesia: *Land Tenure Act, 1969*.

13. The Land Apportionment Act allocated 41 million acres to whites and 44 million to Africans. The Land Tenure Act increased European acres.

14. *A Call to Christians*, Pastoral Message of the Catholic Bishops of Rhodesia, Gwelo, June 5, 1969.

15. *A Crisis of Conscience*, Pastoral Message of the Catholic Bishops of Rhodesia, Salisbury, March 17, 1970.

16. *A Message and Appeal from Church Leaders to the Christian People of Rhodesia*, Salisbury, June 1969, p. 2; italics in the original.

17. United Methodist Church, *Rhodesia 1970*, p. 4.

18. *Washington Post*, January 17, 1972.

19. *Ibid.*

20. *Ibid.*

21. *Ibid.*

22. *New York Times*, January 17, 1971.

23. *Ibid.*

24. *Ibid.*

25. United Methodist Church, *Rhodesia 1970*, p. 4.

26. *Rhodesia Herald*, March 25, 1971.

27. *Ibid.*

28. *Call to Christians*, p. 4.

29. Robert Mugabe and Leopold Takawira are known for their dedication as leaders of the struggling people of Zimbabwe. Robert Mugabe has been in prison detention since 1964 in Salisbury, and Leopold Takawira died in prison in 1970 under very suspicious circumstances.

30. *Crisis of Conscience*.

31. *Ibid.*; emphasis added.

32. *News*, The Methodist Church, p. 1.

33. Rhodesia Methodist Conference, *Statement on Rhodesia*.

CHAPTER 5

The Road to Majority Rule

Majority Rule through Constitutional Means?

A few months before Rhodesia declared itself independent in November 1965, a number of European supporters of Ian Smith, including many school children, wore buttons inscribed with the letters ODB. Smith had stated that Rhodesia would attain majority rule only "over my dead body."

This was a European response to British insistence that Rhodesia would attain independence only on the basis of five principles: (1) that there would be unimpeded progress to majority rule; (2) that there would be guarantees against retrogressive amendment of the Constitution; (3) that there would be immediate improvement in the political status of the African population; (4) that there would be progress towards ending racial discrimination; and (5) that any basis proposed for independence would be acceptable to the people of Rhodesia as a whole.[1] Yet, as we have seen in Chapters 1 and 3, Britain's insistence on these five principles crumbled into the Anglo-Rhodesian Proposed Settlement of 1971, which put the timing of the first principle entirely into the hands of the

Rhodesian government. Through its control of African education and income the government determines how many Africans can qualify for the higher voters' roll, which elects the
majority of seats in the House of Assembly.

It is doubtful that Rhodesia would amend its constitution to
equitably distribute voting privileges, especially since those
who want this distribution do not have the voting power to
make such an amendment. And yet, even if the increase in
African education and salaries continues at the present rate,
there still will not be equal African representation in the
foreseeable future. There is no way majority rule can be attained by African participation in Rhodesia's "constitutional"
system.

Yet, if the attainment of majority rule through constitutional means is impossible, what else is left as a political instrument for the people of Zimbabwe in their struggle for
freedom?

Majority Rule through
British Intervention or Negotiation?

Before the Unilateral Declaration of Independence some
people believed that if the Smith regime rebelled, Britain
would militarily intervene in Rhodesia. UDI was effected and
Britain did not. Then these people revised their thesis and
began to say that if economic sanctions failed to terminate the
state of illegality in Rhodesia, Britain would be forced by
events and by world opinion to intervene militarily in
Rhodesia. But economic sanctions have failed, and Britain has
not intervened. The thesis of British intervention in Rhodesia
is based on a myopic view of Anglo-Rhodesian relations and
on a lack of understanding of British diplomacy.

The British gain nothing in assisting the Africans in Zimbabwe to attain majority rule. In fact they would be worse off
if Rhodesia gained majority rule. Most of the whites in
Rhodesia are blood relatives of the British. If, therefore,

things were to go "wrong" in Zimbabwe under African rule, the Rhodesian whites would most likely run to Britain. The British economy, dilapidated as it is, cannot absorb an influx of Rhodesian whites.

Britain would never intervene militarily in Rhodesia on the side of the Africans against the Europeans. It is very likely that when the balance of forces is changed in Rhodesia to the extent that the Europeans are overpowered by the Africans, Britain will militarily intervene in Rhodesia on the side of the Europeans.

Neither can negotiations produce a settlement that will satisfy Africans. In the process of reaching agreement with Smith the Africans were not consulted at all. Those Africans who met with Sir Alec Douglas-Home were merely told of the Agreement. Such tactics were within what Sir Alec referred to as the "realities of power."

The people of Zimbabwe cannot hope ever to attain majority rule through negotiations with either the Smith regime or the British government or both, for neither recognizes them as parties to the negotiations. They are objects to be negotiated over. The attainment of majority rule through negotiation is impossible.

Majority Rule through Passive Resistance?

Passive resistance has been used as a political instrument with success in some parts of the world, for example in India. The purpose of techniques such as boycotts, strikes, and demonstrations is to break the economic backbone of a country and reap political benefit out of the economic dislocations that follow.

In theory it would seem that such a political instrument could work in Rhodesia. The economy of Rhodesia cannot be run without the participation of the Africans, as shown in Table 5, below. If the 638,000 African employees in the Rhodesian economy went on strike the Rhodesian economy would collapse and the government could collapse as well.

TABLE 5

**RHODESIAN GROSS DOMESTIC PRODUCT BY SECTOR
AND EMPLOYMENT DISTRIBUTION—1965**

Sector	Value (in millions of pounds)	Percent	African Employment	European, Asian, Colored Employment
European Agriculture	45.7	12.9	273,800	4,500
African Agriculture	21.6	6.1	—	—
Mining and Quarrying	24.1	6.8	43,600	2,950
Manufacture	66.6	18.8	71,000	16,130
Building and Construction	15.9	4.5	30,000	5,160
Electricity and Water	14.6	4.1	4,400	1,280
Wholesale and Retail	49.6	14.0	31,700	18,260
Banking, Insurance, Finance	5.2	1.5	2,300	5,680
Real Estate	5.6	1.6	—	—
Ownership of Dwellings	10.1	2.8	—	—
Transport and Communication	30.7	8.7	16,300	10,260
Public Administration and Defence	16.4	4.6	20,100	9,600
Education	11.6	3.3	22,300	5,630
Health	4.1	1.2	6,400	2,800
Domestic Services	10.8	3.0	94,700	350
African Rural Household Services	4.7	1.3	—	—
Other Services	17.2	4.9	21,800	7,180
Total	354.3	100.0	638,000	89,800

Source: *National Accounts and Balance of Payments of Rhodesia, 1968.*

But we must go beyond theoretical assumptions because as a matter of fact the use of a general strike by Africans as a political weapon is not feasible in Rhodesia.

First, for a general strike to succeed in producing even limited results in Rhodesia, it would have to be sustained for at least one month. But the Europeans in Rhodesia control the water and electricity supply to the African townships. In the event of a general strike the regime has not hesitated to shut off this supply. The Africans can do without electricity, but how long can they do without water? These retaliatory measures make it impossible for the African to go on a long strike.[2]

Second, the Rhodesian regime does not take kindly to strikes by Africans. A recent example is the strike effort by Africans at the Shabani asbestos mines. In January 1972 about 400 mine workers went on strike at Shabani. The Rhodesian regime did not ask the Africans why they were striking; it moved in its troops, who fired at the striking miners—killing one African and wounding nine others, according to the regime's figures.[3] Those who are familiar with the reporting of the regime, know that the casualties were higher. As we have seen this policy toward strikes is consistent with the policies of the governments that preceded the present regime.

Demonstrations are another instrument of political action. They include, for example, mass marching, sit-ins, and sleep-ins. But it is illegal in Rhodesia to coerce "the governments by demonstrations, processions, and strikes." We have seen how even the so-called "liberal" governments before 1962 dealt with African demonstrations. When the Rhodesian Front came to power it continued to use the same methods as its predecessors. Demonstrations were met with the show and use of force. The Rhodesia Front government believed that "the African gravitates to the stronger" and that "the crack of the whip" is what Africans understand and appreciate most.[4]

In the Anglo-Rhodesian proposed settlement of November 1971, Smith and Douglas-Home agreed that "the British Government will therefore appoint a commission to ascertain directly from all sections of the population of Rhodesia whether or not these proposals are acceptable and to report accordingly to the British Government."[5] It was further agreed that "in the period before and during the test of acceptability normal political activities will be permitted . . . provided that are conducted in a peaceful and democratic manner."[6] Britain

appointed the Pearce Commission to conduct the test of acceptability of the Anglo-Rhodesian proposals in Rhodesia. The
people of Zimbabwe, who had not been parties to the negotiations that led to these proposals, decided to demonstrate
peacefully to indicate their opposition to this plan which
promised them majority rule only after a period of between
sixty-four and a hundred years. In Gwelo, a town in south-
eastern Rhodesia, more than 10,000 "chanting demonstrators
roared out 'NO' to signal their rejection" of the proposals.[7]
Though unarmed, they were driven back "by armed mobile
police units and police reservists, backed by heavily armed
troops."[8] The government reported one death and many in-
juries. In Umtali in eastern Rhodesia thousands of African
demonstrators attempted to march peacefully into the city to
register their opposition to the Anglo-Rhodesian proposals.
They were unarmed, and yet police opened fire and killed at
least eight.[9] In Salisbury thousands of African demonstrators
marched into the city to protest the proposals. They too were
unarmed, and yet the police opened fire, killing at least three
Africans and wounding many more.[10] In Fort Victoria and
Shabani in southern Rhodesia the police opened fire on peaceful demonstrators, killing at least one African and wounding
many more.

The Rhodesian regime attempted to explain that the police
had opened fire "after" the Africans had rioted. This is not
true. Indeed there were riots in Rhodesia during January
1972. But the riots began only as a result of police opening fire
and killing unarmed Africans. As Charles Mohr of the *New
York Times* reported, "Thousands of blacks showed up, clog-
ging halls, stairs and sidewalks and presumably putting 'NO'
on the forms." He goes on to report that "white Rhodesians
were furious because the method seemed to be a form of
ballot."[11] But the Africans had been explicitly invited to express their opinion; for doing so they became shooting targets
of the Rhodesian armed forces.

The history of African attempts at passive resistance has
been one of constant government suppression. It is clear that

the white regime can and will control such attempts through either its economic sanctions or its police intervention. It has not failed to use either in the past; it may be presumed that the future will be no different. The African can only conclude that majority rule cannot be attained in Zimbabwe through passive resistance.

The Other Alternative

Rhodesia's future is grim and has gone beyond the point where it can be salvaged without the worst expression of race hatred. The longer the white minority regime stays in power the grimmer the future of Rhodesia becomes. In the immediate future the Rhodesian regime will definitely become more oppressive. The rejection of the Anglo-Rhodesian settlement by the African people has galvanized the more extreme elements of the already extreme Rhodesian white society. The extreme right wing of Smith's Rhodesian Front was as violently opposed to the settlement as the Africans were. During the Pearce Commission exercise about one thousand right-wingers held a meeting to organize the basis for a new government. Further, the riots and disturbances that accompanied African rejection of the settlement are said to have angered the conservative majority of whites. This led to the formation of the new Rhodesia National Party composed of extreme right-wing dissidents from among former Rhodesia Front members.

If he is to survive in Rhodesian politics, Ian Smith has no alternative but to accommodate the elements in the white society which have begun criticizing him. Although since 1965 it had been considered heretical in Rhodesia to criticize Smith, the situation changed when he failed to settle with Britain without visible political opposition from the Africans. Smith is now criticized, first of all, for having allowed the Africans to be consulted on the Anglo-Rhodesian settlement. To silence these European critics, his regime must become more oppressive. If he is slow in tightening the chains around the Africans he will be removed from power. Smith himself helped topple Winston Field, the first Rhodesian Front prime minister, when Field refused to lead the rebellion against Britain. Should Smith refuse to be more oppressive than he has already been, the cup which he made Field taste will be passed to his own lips.

But whether Smith stays in power or not, the Rhodesian regime will become more oppressive than ever. Rhodesian Europeans are a terrified people. They are secure only when they see the African completely submissive and their authority unchallenged. The African resistance of January 1972, after seven years of relative peace and quiet, has challenged this security. The reaction of Rhodesian whites today is one of fear.

Beyond the immediate future the European will more and more be forced to fight for his own survival, and the odds are against him. Oppression itself fosters hatred, and hatred drives human beings to extreme actions. Many Africans have begun actually to hate the white men in Rhodesia. Should that hatred be accompanied by some patriotic and nationalist flavor, not even their guns will save the white men in Rhodesia. Sir Roy Welensky, the former Prime Minister of the Federation of Rhodesia and Nyasaland, said in reference to the disturbances of January 1972 that "the grass had to be dry enough to burn."[12] The Europeans of Rhodesia can continue to rule the African of Zimbabwe only as long as the African is not willing to pay the price of his freedom. Now the "grass is dry," and the African is willing to pay the price.

But the European of Rhodesia is not going to give up easily. He will stand and fight because at least one-third of the European population has no home other than Rhodesia. He cannot be expected to give up what he regards as the fruit of his labor. He is prepared to do anything to maintain the *status quo* and his own survival. He is aware of his numerical disadvantage, but he puts his confidence in military superiority. Should the need arise, it should not be doubted that the white man in

Rhodesia is prepared to mow down with bullets as many Africans as it takes to assert white supremacy.

Racial conflict is inevitable. Two races are fighting for survival. As the days pass the animosity between them increases. And time is on the side of the Africans. There is nothing the European can do to overcome the numerical superiority of the Africans or end their hostility. Even if the European relaxed his oppression and gave the African more rights, including voting power, the African would overthrow the minority regime by the use of the ballot. If, as seems more likely, the European tightens the oppression, he will increase the hostility of the Africans and drive them to revolution. Either way the European loses. But since it seems there is no way the Africans can overcome their oppression by peaceful means, Rhodesia will not be able to escape violence.

The struggle is shaping into two forms: the spontaneous eruption of the masses and the organization of revolutionaries.

The Spontaneous Struggle of the Masses

Masses of people remain oppressed only as long as they do not gain some political consciousness. And yet oppression itself generates that consciousness. When the masses are deprived of what they hold dear, it is only a matter of time before they revolt.

In January 1972 the British government and the Smith regime—working on the assumption that the Africans were passive—attempted to sell the Anglo-Rhodesian proposed settlement to the Africans; they dispatched the Pearce Commission to Rhodesia to test the opinion of the people. As Charles Mohr of the *New York Times* reported, both the British government and the Smith regime "regarded the work of the opinion commission a mere formality, almost certain to result in a finding of approval for the proposals."[13] They were taken by surprise. The Africans from all corners of Zimbabwe spontaneously came out in large numbers and vehemently demonstrated that the Anglo-Rhodesian terms were unacceptable to them. Mohr reported,

> Urban blacks had been generally expected to oppose the pro-posals, but more than 80 per cent of blacks live on the tribal trust lands under the authority of 200 chiefs on the Government's payroll. It had been thought that chiefs, tribal councils and the population there would generally give their approval, possibly under the influence of white district offi-cers. In fact tribal blacks were as adamant as urban blacks. So far only one chief, with 19,000 followers, has expressed approval.[14]

There was no indication that the Africans had been or-ganized. The African National Council (ANC) was not formed until December 1971, and since the banning of ZANU and ZAPU in August 1964, no African political or-ganization had operated within the country. The ANC could not have organized all these demonstrations against the Anglo-Rhodesian proposals within one month. Foreign reporters in Rhodesia who observed the operations of the Pearce Commission came to the conclusion that the Africans were not intimidated by anyone into demonstrating against the proposals. "In virtually every case the people refused. But no one has yet offered any credible proof that there exists a significant number of blacks who want to approve the propos-als who are intimidated," the *New York Times* reporter wrote.[15]

When the Smith regime encountered the Africans with gunfire and arrests, the Africans did not retreat. They met violence with violence. They rioted, threw stones, burned buildings and cars. The riots of January 1972 were very dif-ferent from those of July 1960. In 1960 the Africans tended to respond to police violence with violence against African prop-erty and the persons of fellow Africans. But in January 1972 the Africans directed their violence to European property and persons. No European was hurt in 1960, but in 1972 a number of Europeans were hospitalized, some with fractured skulls. In 1960 the riots were contained mainly in the African town-ships. But in 1972 the Africans aimed at getting to the city centers, the sanctuaries of the Europeans. The *Washington Post* reported, "Some gangs raided into Salisbury itself, smashing car windows and stoning passing cars only a mile from the city center."[16] The *Post* also reported, "An estimated 8,000 demonstrators, apparently attempting to invade the predominantly white center of Gwelo, were finally turned back by repeated tear gas attacks launched by armed mobile police units and police reservists, backed by heavily armed troops."[17] Attacks by African demonstrators on the Europeans and their sanctuaries were unheard of before 1972.

What the events of the early months of 1972 demonstrated was that the people of Zimbabwe had become politically conscious enough to identify the enemy; they responded to the regime's violence against them by violence against the section of the population that sustained the oppressive regime. As long as the Africans are oppressed, the Europeans of Rhodesia will remain the target of the spontaneous action of the masses. The European of Rhodesia cannot live secure when he knows that his African cook, his African baby-sitter, his African garden "boy," and his African chauffeur are unpredictable. *Time* put the situation mildly when it wrote, "Servants usually know their masters, someone once observed, but masters seldom know their servants. The thesis has been overwhelmingly proved during the past six weeks in Rhodesia, where the white man is customarily called 'boss' and the black man 'boy.' "[18]

Spontaneous political struggle serves two functions. First, it demonstrates the consciousness of the masses, which, however, must be developed if the political struggle is to be effectively channelled. Secondly, spontaneous action serves to harass the political opponent and force him to spread his forces thinly. For example, because of the spontaneous demonstrations and subsequent riots that erupted all over Zimbabwe in 1972, the Smith regime was forced to withdraw some of its armed units from the Zambezi Valley, where they were patrolling the Rhodesian border with Zambia. The regime was also forced to cancel or postpone some meetings of the Pearce Commission because it had not enough police and armed units to deal with the spontaneous actions of the masses.

However, spontaneous political struggle very rarely achieves its objectives if it is not carried out in conjunction with other forms of action. Its greatest weakness is that it cannot be programmed. It may not occur when there is need for it, or it may occur when it should be postponed. It may not occur all over the country simultaneously. The Smith regime was able to suppress the Tangwena people in Zimbabwe in 1969 mainly because they were not supported with similar acts of resistance in other parts of the country. It is vital that the spontaneous actions of the masses of Zimbabwe be brought into coordination with organized resistance to the Smith regime; the organized resistance must always be prepared to take advantage of the spontaneity of the masses and even to encourage it.

Organized Resistance

Colonialism was routed out of most parts of Africa mainly through the organized resistance of the African people. But Rhodesia differs from most other African countries in that one-third of its white population is native-born. Rhodesia has Europeans—including Ian Smith himself—who have known no other home than Rhodesia. Thus, scare tactics against these Europeans cannot usher in majority rule, for such tactics can work only on people who can pack their bags and say, "We are going back home." The Europeans will fight for their Rhodesia just as the Africans will fight to establish their Zimbabwe. Events of the past years have demonstrated that the two races cannot coexist. The partnership of races that was tried in the Federation of Rhodesia and Nyasaland was the partnership of a horse and rider. It failed.

To speak of organized resistance in Zimbabwe is not to

speak of scare tactics but of the organization of revolutionaries. Before 1966 there were isolated incidents of petrol bombs exploding in some part of Zimbabwe, and the African leadership predicted a holocaust descending upon the Europeans of Rhodesia. But for years such a holocaust did not appear. While threats of this kind have been effective in struggles for freedom throughout other parts of the African continent, they did not work in Rhodesia, and the Europeans became more entrenched than ever.

After years of frustration and failure in their political struggle Zimbabweans have begun to think in terms of a revolution that goes beyond firing shots in the Zambezi Valley, far away from European centers. But there are many difficulties to be faced before a revolution can be prosecuted in Zimbabwe, including the development of true revolutionaries. To an analysis of these difficulties we now turn.

NOTES

1. *Southern Rhodesia: Documents Relating to the Negotiations Between the United Kingdom and Rhodesia Governments, November 1963–November 1965*. London, HMSO, CMND 2807.

2. African townships are built in such a way that the government can easily isolate one township from another and thus control the people within each township.

3. See *Daily Telegraph* (London), January 14, 1972.

4. A. Skeen, *Prelude to Independence*, p. 52.

5. *Proposals for a Settlement*, 1971, p. 11.

6. *Ibid.*

7. *Washington Post*, January 19, 1972.

8. *Ibid.*, January 18, 1972.

9. *Ibid.*, January 22, 1972.

10. *New York Times*, January 21, 1972.

11. *Ibid.*, January 24, 1972.

12. *Washington Post*, January 1972.

13. *New York Times*, January 24, 1972.

14. *Ibid.*

15. *Ibid.*

16. *Washington Post*, January 20, 1972.

17. *Ibid.*, January 18, 1972.

18. *Time*, March 6, 1972, p. 30.

CHAPTER 6

The Difficulties of
Revolution in Zimbabwe

The obstacles to revolution in Zimbabwe are many. Like Lenin, Zimbabweans are faced not only with the question "What is to be done?" but also "Where to begin?" What has happened in Zimbabwe since December 1972 demonstrates that the Zimbabweans are beginning to comprehend the objective conditions of Zimbabwe. Prior to December 1972 such understanding was greatly lacking. The Zimbabweans will succeed in their revolution only if they act on an accurate perception of the objective realities of their situation.

Seven factors must be comprehended before the revolution can succeed: (1) the state of mind of the Zimbabweans, (2) the leadership, (3) the attempt from 1960 to prosecute a revolution without an ideology, (4) the attempt to prosecute a revolution without revolutionaries, (5) the nature of exile politics, which has bogged down the efforts to wage a revolution, (6) the political opportunism which infiltrates every revolution, and (7) the international dimensions of the Rhodesian problem.

The State of Mind of the Zimbabweans

For the African in Rhodesia life has always been a struggle for survival, because all the means of livelihood are under the control of the European. This very struggle for self-preservation created, until recently, a state of mind that is antithetic to the success of a political struggle.

For example, on March 30, 1972, the Rhodesian regime announced that 5,000 unemployed Africans in Harare Township alone would be returned to their rural homes.[1] R.C. Biggs, the then Director of African Administration, followed this with another shocking statement: "Married men in the township who had jobs would be 'advised' to return their dependents to their homes."[2] And yet, as we have already seen, the Land Apportionment Act, the Land Tenure Act, and the Land Husbandry Act have deprived thousands of the Africans of any land to return to. In towns there are not enough jobs, and in the rural areas there is not enough land. Those who are fortunate enough to get jobs or to be admitted to schools have, until recently, tended to hold fast to what they had, knowing that if they let it go the alternative would be starvation. Such a state of affairs created in Zimbabweans a state of mind that drove thousands to compromise with the system that held an axe over their necks.

At school almost every African student who managed to get up to grade 12 had to accept certain humiliations. He had to eat beans infested with worms and insects; he had to drink milk that had been mixed with water for his dinner. He knew that if he went on strike he would be expelled from school and would find himself with reduced prospects for employment and without land in rural areas. He had to submit to the school authorities in order to have at least a fighting chance for a better future. That submission itself did not leave the mind untouched.

The African student has constantly been told that he is

one of the few fortunate Africans to receive an education. He has constantly been led to believe that he is the best, the elite. He has been taught that to speak English is a sign of sophistication and civilization. Gradually the African student accepted this brainwashing. I do not know of a single meeting of Zimbabwean students in Zimbabwe or abroad that has not been conducted in English, even if all speak the same African language.

The African student has been taught to despise his fellow African. He has come to believe that Africans without education are inferior to him, and he has thus accepted the "superiority" of the European over the African. Such a man cannot fight a revolution. He needs "de-brainwashing."

After receiving eight, twelve, or more years of education, this African goes to the urban areas and works for and under the European. He sticks to his job, faithfully serving his European master. He begins to talk of *Murungu Wangu* ("my European"). Such a man cannot engage in any political action against the Europeans of Rhodesia; he admires them too much to be politically effective. Fortunately for Zimbabwe these Africans comprise not more than 20 percent of the African population. But even 20 percent is too high. It is these Africans who have delayed the Zimbabwean revolution.

Unfortunately, most attempts at politicization until recently were aimed only at urban and educated Africans. Of all the African political organizations in Zimbabwe, only the African National Congress (1957–1959) organized the rural areas and carried out rural political activities. All the others—the National Democratic Party (1960), the Zimbabwe African People's Union (1961), the Zimbabwe African National Union (1963–64), and the People's Caretaker Council (1963–64)—were urban based with very little efficient organization in the rural areas. What the Zimbabwe politicians misperceived until very recently was the correlation between education and the level of politicization; they mistook education as a sign of politicization. And yet a person with a Ph.D. can remain unpoliticized while one who never saw a schoolhouse door can be highly politicized. The urban Africans went to mass political rallies, listened to the political speeches, applauded the man who spoke the best English, and went home to business as usual.

While Zimbabwean politicians delivered their brilliant English speeches, the Rhodesian regime became more oppressive. The status of the urban African did not improve; in fact it deteriorated. Then in 1972 the urban African worker was "advised" to send his dependents to his rural home. Those who thought that they were safe at their jobs began losing them and saw the European regime replacing Africans with white immigrants. In 1966 alone 9,000 indigenous Africans in Rhodesia lost their jobs while no European lost his. This was after 16,000 "alien" Africans had already been dismissed. By 1967 about 20,000 indigenous Africans had lost their jobs, and none of the 48,000 Africans who reached the age of sixteen in 1967 and were not absorbed into the schools got a job; yet the European level of employment remained constant.[3] The Rhodesian regime went even further and displaced Africans from their rural homes to make room for white farmers.[4] The people of Zimbabwe, educated and uneducated, urban dwellers and rural residents, began to receive a new political consciousness. Oppression itself was now politicizing the people of Zimbabwe. Those who had not been motivated before began to be ripe for the revolution.

Thus oppression breeds revolutionary consciousness. Even urban Zimbabweans have begun to realize that they are not secure as long as the European rules Zimbabwe. Even the African chiefs who had for expediency hobnobbed with the Rhodesian regimes and enjoyed the benefits that came from such a relationship have begun to repudiate their past. The demonstrations and riots of January 1972 and the support the guerrillas have been given since December 1972 attest to this change in the state of mind of the Zimbabweans.

African Leadership

Leaders emerge from the people. Thus in most cases, though by no means all, leaders of a political movement reflect the state of mind of the followers. The Zimbabwe political leadership has always emerged from the urban people, and like most of the followers the leaders have been victims of the subtle brainwashing process.

Before 1960 the Africans of Zimbabwe did not think in terms of wresting power from the hands of the Europeans. The tendency of the educated Africans was to join organizations that sought to improve their conditions of life. They wanted relaxation of liquor laws, the right to use hotels, and relaxation of discrimination. Thus a number of highly educated men such as Joshua Nkomo, Enoch Dumbutshena, S. T. J. Samkange, and Leopold Takawira joined multiracial organizations like the African Welfare Societies, the Capricorn African Society, and the Inter-Racial Association.[5] These are the people who took up the political leadership of the people of Zimbabwe. Their struggle then was directed against racial discrimination and not toward majority rule in Zimbabwe. In fact the struggle was directed towards the improvement of living conditions for the educated people.

On September 12, 1957, the African National Congress (ANC) was born, led by Joshua Nkomo, James Chikerema, George Nyandoro, and others. Again, the objective of these leaders was to improve the well-being of the African, to fight against discrimination. The targets of their political activities were laws such as the Land Apportionment Act and the Land

Husbandry Act. They also sought to improve the conditions of life of rural people. They successfully aroused the rural people and led their fight for the right to own more land and cattle. The ANC was a protest movement. Its protest frightened the Europeans, and it was banned on February 25, 1959, although the ANC leaders never talked of majority rule.

On January 1, 1960 the National Democratic Party (NDP) was formed, led by Michael Mawema and later by Joshua Nkomo, Ndabaningi Sithole, Robert Mugabe, and others. These leaders, though very brilliant men with the interest of the Zimbabwe people at heart, failed to perceive that the struggle in Zimbabwe would have to take a form different from the independence struggle in other African countries. In African colonies like the Gold Goast, Nigeria, Tanganyika, and Uganda the struggle was against British colonialism. In Rhodesia the struggle was against European settlerism backed by British colonialism. The Europeans never intended to remain in the Gold Coast or in Nigeria; in Rhodesia they were there to stay.

However, the NDP differed from the ANC. The NDP began campaigning for majority rule in Zimbabwe. But the leaders of the NDP thought the independence of Zimbabwe would be won around a constitutional conference table and not on the battlefield. After all, Ghana had attained its independence in 1957 through constitutional talks backed by tactics of harassment; Nigeria had won its independence in 1960 through the same means. Everywhere in Africa leaders of independence movements were demanding constitutional conferences with the colonial powers. The Zimbabwe leaders followed suit and demanded a constitutional conference to pave the way for majority rule. The NDP leaders pressured Britain to call for such a conference; between November 20, 1960 and early January 1961 Joshua Nkomo, the President of the NDP, flew to London three times.[6] The NDP leadership saw London as the battleground, and they succeeded in making Britain put pressure on the Rhodesian government to accept the idea of a constitutional conference. Indeed, Prime Minister Sir Edgar Whitehead also wanted a constitutional conference because he wanted the 1923 Constitution, in which Britain had reserved powers to intervene in Rhodesian internal affairs, to be scrapped and replaced by a constitution in which Britain had no such powers.

Britain called a Constitutional Conference in London which was quickly adjourned to Salisbury by the end of January 1961. The NDP had two delegates, Joshua Nkomo and Ndabaningi Sithole, and two advisers, Herbert Chitepo and George Silundika. The people of Zimbabwe put all their hopes in this Conference and all their confidence in their leaders. Their representatives at the conference were learned gentlemen: Joshua Nkomo had a degree in social work and Ndabaningi Sithole a divinity degree; Herbert Chitepo was at that time the best legal mind the Africans could produce; and George Silundika had some university education. The people of Zimbabwe had thought education was equivalent to political ingenuity. Most Zimbabweans have lived to regret the day they were represented by these men in this Conference.

When it came to hard bargaining the African leaders found themselves at the mercy of Duncan Sandys, the deft British minister in charge of the Conference. They were presented with a draft Constitution in which the Africans would have fifteen seats in a parliament of sixty-five. At the time the Conference was being held no African had ever been allowed to sit in the Rhodesian Parliament. One could imagine what an attraction these fifteen seats became to the African leaders who had witnessed African leaders elsewhere in Africa becoming Members of Parliament. At the time of the Conference Northern Rhodesia had nine Africans in a Parliament of thirty, and Nyasaland had twenty Africans in a Parliament of thirty-three.

The NDP delegation, had received a mandate from the party's Executive Council to demand "one man–one vote" for the franchise in the new Constitution and nothing less.

It thus found itself torn between the mandate and the offer of fifteen African seats plus the Bill of Rights which Britain and the Rhodesian government had agreed to insert into the Constitution. To get out of the trap the delegation formulated a vague position. They said they would neither accept nor reject the draft Constitution, but they would not put obstacles in the way of its implemenation. Britain took this as acceptance of the draft Constitution. Addressing about 30,000 people on March 19, 1961, Joshua Nkomo himself said, "We were able to move the mountain which had been set before us an inch by getting the declaration of human rights and the protection of the courts enshrined in the new Constitution."[7] Joshua Nkomo and his delegation lived to see that neither the Bill of Rights nor the courts of Rhodesia were designed to protect the African in any way.

Soon after the Constitutional Conference had come to an end the NDP leaders found themselves at each other's throats. Some, like Michael Mawema, Leopold Takawira, and Enos Nkala, believed the NDP delegation had betrayed the mandate of the party. Meeting after meeting of the NDP branches began repudiating the proposed Constitution, and the entire NDP delegation began to claim that it had never accepted the whole Constitution, but only certain parts, like the Bill of Rights. The NDP conference held on June 17–18, 1961 in Bulawayo rejected the whole Constitution. In October 1961 the Party decided not to participate in any elections held under this Constitution.

If the NDP leaders had displayed qualities of leadership they would either have carried out the mandate of the party at the Constitutional Conference and refused to accept any constitution that did not include the principle of adult suffrage; or, once they had betrayed that mandate by implying acceptance of the Constitution, they would have tried to convince the party of whatever advantages, if any, they had found in the Constitution. But, lacking political insight, they instead again put their hopes on Britain. Joshua Nkomo resumed his trips to London and around the world. A quick look at the

Rhodesian press, including the *Daily News* (Salisbury), which was very favorable to Nkomo, indicates how frequently Nkomo travelled. On February 13, 1961 he flew to London. In late February he flew to Cairo, Addis Ababa, and Damascus. In early March he flew to London. On March 20 he flew to Nairobi and Cairo and in mid-April to London and Milan. It had not yet occurred to the NDP President that the fight must be waged on home ground. If the NDP leadership wanted to sack the 1961 Constitution either before or after it was implemented, they should not have turned to London. Only the people of Zimbabwe could do it. The leadership should have concentrated on organizing the people; they should have utilized the time, money, and energy which they were expending abroad to build a strong party in constant touch with the grass roots.

Hoping that scare tactics would force Britain to rescind the 1961 Constitution, the NDP leaders unleashed verbal attacks on Britain and organized a referendum of their own on the Constitution. In the NDP referendum an impressive 372,546 votes were cast against the Constitution and 471 were cast in favor of it.[8] In the official referendum 41,949 votes were cast in favor of the Constitution and 21,846 against it.[9] Shortly after the two referendums, Joshua Nkomo again flew to London with the NDP referendum results, but to his surprise the British government was unimpressed. NDP leaders attempted to organize strikes and picketing, but Sir Edgar Whitehead banned the party on December 9, 1961.

Nine days after the ban, the leaders regrouped and formed the Zimbabwe African People's Union (ZAPU). The same old faces, Joshua Nkomo, Ndabaningi Sithole, Robert Mugabe, and J.Z. Moyo, reappeared as executives of the new party. The aims and objectives of the party were the same as those of the NDP. ZAPU was demanding majority rule just as the NDP had demanded it. One might have expected the ZAPU leadership to have learned from the NDP experience and to adopt new tactics to attain this objective. Had the leadership believed in the ability of themselves and the other Africans to wage and win their own struggle, these leaders would have concentrated on organizing the Zimbabweans. But instead the leadership decided to shift their pressure tactics a step farther away from Zimbabwe. Since they had failed to make Britain abrogate the 1961 Constitution, they turned to the United Nations to do it for them. They decided to pressure the UN to pressure Britain to pressure the Rhodesian government to turn political power over to the Africans.

However, the ZAPU leaders were led to these bankrupt tactics because in the 1960's the United Nations had seemed to offer great hope to the peoples of Africa. In 1960 the UN had adopted General Assembly Resolution 1514 (XV), the "United Nations Declaration on the Granting of Independence to Colonial Countries and Peoples." The UN was assisting in the decolonization of Trusteeship Territories like Tanganyika, Burundi, Rwanda, and Togo. ZAPU leaders, unmindful of the fact that Rhodesia was not a Trusteeship Territory but a settler colony, placed their hopes in the UN. Joshua Nkomo flew to New York to address the United Nations Committee on Decolonization in April 1962 while on a prolonged trip around the world.[10] He flew again to New York in July, and when he returned to Zimbabwe he said that he had come "to launch his final and decisive offensive against settler domination."[11] The ZAPU leadership declared that African majority rule would be achieved in 1962. As early as February 1962, ZAPU officials began telling ZAPU branches all over the country that "Mr. Nkomo will be Prime Minister this year in October."[12] Joshua Nkomo was in the habit of telling crowds each time he returned from abroad that "independence is just around the corner." Zimbabweans expected liberation soon. They refused to believe that their leader was making all those trips for nothing.

Immediately after the NDP debacle at the Constitutional Conference voices of reason began to be heard in Zimbabwe. Michael Mawema and Patrick Matimba formed their own party called the Zimbabwe National Party (ZNP). The ZNP

leadership warned, "We do not expect the UN to fight our battle for us. The UN is comprised of imperialists, fascists, Nazis, Communists and Nationalists. The UN has never liquidated colonialism in any country. It is just an international Cooling Chamber."[13] Instead of being listened to, the ZNP leaders were castigated, beaten up, and declared traitors. Their voices were drowned under the terror unleashed against them by the ZAPU leaders.

However ZAPU seemed, at least superficially, to be well organized and a threat to the regime's stability. Thus Sir Edgar Whitehead banned the party on September 20, 1962 and jailed the leaders. Scattered riots occurred all over the country, but since the ZAPU leaders had not organized an efficient underground movement the riots quickly fizzled out under police brutality. Between September 1962 and June 1963 there was no organized political activity by the people of Zimbabwe. Elections were held in December 1962 without any significant effort to disrupt them. Most African voters boycotted the elections, and the Rhodesian Front was elected to power. Immediately after the elections the RF government released all African political detainees as a gesture of good will. Shortly after their release all the senior leaders of the banned ZAPU fled to Tanganyika.

A false atmosphere of hope perverted the minds of Zimbabwean politicians and their followers. Radio broadcasts from Tanganyika declared that the leaders would fight from abroad to usher majority rule into Zimbabwe, and the people of Zimbabwe believed them. The leaders felt that since the Rhodesian regime had become very oppressive and was banning all African political movements, the revolution could be fought more effectively from exile. But after a short while the Zimbabweans heard from Tanganyika that the leaders were fighting each other. In June 1963 the leaders split, with Joshua Nkomo leading one faction and Ndabaningi Sithole the other. Instead of coming home to Zimbabwe to explain why they were breaking from Nkomo, whom they had so strongly supported, the Sithole group toured African countries to mobilize, they said, the support of African leaders. It seems they did not realize that before they mobilized the leaders of independent African countries they should mobilize the people of Zimbabwe. It was in Zimbabwe—not in Ghana, Tanganyika, or Nigeria—that the struggle had to be fought and won. However, in July 1963 members of both groups began to flock back to Zimbabwe to put their cases before the people and presumably to let the people decide which group was their legitimate representative.

The period between June 1963 and August 1964 is one of which every Zimbabwean should be ashamed. Brother turned against brother, son against father, sister against sister. Families were broken add friendships ended, and the objective of the political struggle was forgotten. In August 1963 the Sithole group formed the Zimbabwe African National Union (ZANU) and the Nkomo group formed the People's Caretaker Council (PCC), which outside Zimbabwe called itself ZAPU. Instead of waging the struggle against the Rhodesian political system, the two groups incited their youth to attack each other and beat or even kill any African who seemed to support the rival group. For fifteen months the Rhodesian Europeans felt secure while every African in Zimbabwe lived in fear of fellow Africans. No words written or spoken can express the terror, the tears, and the blood of these fifteen months of misguided leadership.

The leaderships of PCC and ZANU worked from a philosophy, if it can be called such, borrowed from an African saying that when you are faced with a snake in your own house and a lion outside the house you must fight the snake before you tackle the lion. The Rhodesian government encouraged these misguided activities of the Zimbabwe leaders. It reduced the strength of the police force in African townships and made very few arrests of Africans for killing fellow Africans. After fifteen months the regime banned the two parties and tried to appear to the African people as their savior from the claws of disaster engineered by the African leaders.

The political mismanagement of the African leaders of Zimbabwe and their myopic approach to Rhodesian politics before June 1963 can be forgiven if we see these miscalculations in context: other African colonies were achieving their independence without revolution; they had only to put pressure on their colonial powers. The United Nations seemed to give hope to the African peoples, so misplaced confidence in the UN is understandable. But the miseries the leaders caused the people of Zimbabwe between June 1963 and August 1964 are inexcusable.

There is reason to believe that the people of Zimbabwe have learned from their miseries. They know what divisions can do to a struggling people. Leaders who worked for PCC or ZANU and tried to liquidate each other are again working together in the new African National Council. In 1972 they performed a superb job. The errors of the past should not continue to dog the politics of Zimbabwe but should be utilized as courses in the school of experience.

Revolution without Ideology

Revolution is not necessarily synonymous with firing a gun, for where it is necessary to seize political power by the use of force, the gunfire comes only at a very advanced stage. Revolution is a process that requires discipline of the mind and body and determination of the spirit. It requires direction of purpose and goes beyond the mere seizure of political power. In short, it requires an ideology, a set of ideas that are adhered to and in whose framework action is carried out.

Until very recently no Zimbabwean political organization has ever had a set of theories or ideas which provided the framework for action. The cry was, "Majority Rule NOW," but no one realized that the attainment of majority rule would require discipline and determination; no one said what would happen after majority rule. ZANU published a Yellow Book of Policy and Principles, which promised socialism in Zimbabwe.[14] But the principles in the Yellow Book were hastily drawn up and very cryptic. They fell short of being an ideology.

Since the leaders of Zimbabwe had never thought of attaining power in Zimbabwe through a revolution and since they were preoccupied with the desire to replace white rulers with black rulers, they never thought of developing an ideology. It was not until the banning of ZANU and the PCC in August 1964 that the leaders of Zimbabwe realized that political power in Zimbabwe would not be transferred to the African people on a silver platter. They had to fight for it. Only then did they begin to talk of a revolution.

But by that time they were operating under heavy pressure. Since the parties had been banned in Rhodesia, they had to operate from exile. PCC in exile called itself ZAPU; ZANU in exile established the Zimbabwe National Liberation Army (ZNLA). The first problem both ZAPU and ZANU had to face was how to export a revolution from exile into Zimbabwe, where they had left no organizational infrastructure. Their bases were in Zambia, separated from the home ground by the great Zambezi River, and in Tanzania. The second difficulty both ZAPU and ZANU had to overcome was one which they created for themselves when they told the people of Zimbabwe that victory was "just around the corner." Before the split of the original ZAPU the leaders had aroused the expectations of the people, who now were waiting for the results. ZANU had split from Joshua Nkomo because, as the ZANU leaders said, Nkomo had failed to deliver the promised goods. This therefore meant that if ZANU was to maintain its *raison d'être*, it had to demonstrate to the people of Zimbabwe that it could deliver the cherished majority rule. But the fratricidal struggle between ZANU and PCC prevented ZANU from working for this goal. Nevertheless both ZANU and ZAPU (PCC) in exile continued to claim that they would deliver results to the people of Zimbabwe.

Revolution without Revolutionaries

Such a state of affairs created a third difficulty. ZANU and ZAPU in exile began to compete with each other for legitimacy in the eyes of Zimbabweans at home. They began to undermine each other, each claiming to be fighting in Zimbabwe and inflicting damages on the Smith forces. To fight militarily in Zimbabwe both ZANU and ZAPU needed money and military hardware, for which they depended on the Organization of African Unity and friendly states. But to put pressure on the donors, ZANU and ZAPU had to appear to be fighting. Thus fighting was sometimes initiated by both ZANU and ZAPU not necessarily for revolutionary effectiveness but for the sake of appearing to be involved in liberation activity.

The leaders of the revolution were earnest men but, until recently, not revolutionaries. Herbert Chitepo and James Chikerema, the respective leaders of ZANU and ZAPU in exile, could not by any definition have been called, in 1964, revolutionaries.[15] They were ardent nationalists but not revolutionaries. A nationalist is a person who loves his motherland and its people. A revolutionary is a person who loves his motherland and its people and struggles effectively to bring about political, social, and economic changes for their benefit. Both Chitepo and Chikerema have always loved Zimbabwe. But neither of them in 1964 had a political, social, or economic program to liberate Zimbabwe from the decay it has been experiencing. In 1964 neither had any training in guerrilla warfare or in revolution in general. And yet they had to lead the revolution of Zimbabwe. Between 1964 and 1970 the Zimbabwe revolution was a revolution without an ideology and a revolution without revolutionaries. The results were disastrous. Failure after failure demoralized the fighting forces, and leaders quarrelled and split.

Between 1964 and 1970 many dedicated men died fighting in Zimbabwe. Eshmael Mlambo, in his *Rhodesia: The Struggle for a Birth Right*, attempts to put together from press reports the figures of Zimbabwean fighting men who died in the line of service.[16] The Zimbabweans who died in this struggle are heroes of Zimbabwe, and shrines will be built in their honor in the land for which they shed their blood and laid down their lives. But we must ask if their lives could have been put to better use in the revolution of Zimbabwe.

The fighting men of Zimbabwe were sent to fight amid a population that had not been mentally prepared to accept and support a revolution. The general public did not know what its role was in guerrilla warfare—what it was expected to do and how to resist police pressure and avoid surrendering the guerrillas. ZANU and ZAPU had put emphasis on gunfire rather than on the revolutionary infrastructure that would have made the gunfire effective. As a result, many guerrillas failed to get sufficient protection and support from the general public. They ended up in the hands of Rhodesian police. For example, in April 1966 seven well-trained and determined men entered Rhodesia with specific instructions to carry out some revolutionary acts. In the words of freedom fighter George Kanyemba, one of the seven, " . . . before we could start our mission, we were captured."[17] In June 1966 seven other guerrillas successfully carried out their mission but failed to get sufficient protection from the local populace; thus they were arrested before they could escape.[18]

In some cases guerrilla activities were brilliantly executed but failed to arouse the unprepared Africans to increased support for the guerrillas. For example, a single guerrilla, Joshua Werekwere, performed a number of revolutionary acts in Salisbury itself between April and August 1965.[19] In

Wankie two youths performed acts because "their hearts were 'very sore' with the Government."[20] Many more acts were performed all over Zimbabwe, and yet the masses were not aroused. ZANU and ZAPU had not prepared the minds of the people. These acts would have had great impact in the revolution if the revolutionary preparation had been done before the acts were performed.

The incidents at Hartley and Karoi show how effective the Zimbabwe revolutionary acts could have been had the people been prepared to support and follow up the activities of the guerrillas. At the end of May 1966 a group of guerrillas performed acts in Hartley on two European supporters of the Rhodesian regime, Mr. and Mrs. J.H. Viljoen.[21] On June 4, 1966, an African cook in Karoi, Pearce Jokore, who had suffered injustice from his European employers, working for months without pay, was so inspired by the acts in Hartley that he decided to avenge himself on the three Europeans who had exploited him.[22] Karoi is about eighty-two miles from Hartley. If ZANU and ZAPU had captured the minds of all Zimbabweans in such a way that they would respond as Jokore did, Zimbabwe would have been free a long time ago. Each guerrilla activity would have had long linkage effects with tremendous results.

It is a principle of guerrilla warfare that if the revolution must be waged with minimum resources, each revolutionary act must cause ripples and achieve maximum results. This can be done only if the masses recognize the message of each guerrilla activity and immediately know what they are expected to do.

ZANU and ZAPU violated another principle of guerrilla warfare. Guerrilla units should as much as possible avoid direct confrontation with the enemy's superior force. Guerrilla units are generally not as well armed as regular forces and are usually fewer in number. In any confrontation between the enemy's regular forces and the guerrilla units, the revolutionary forces are nearly always at a great disadvantage, and thus such a confrontation must be avoided. ZANU and ZAPU occasionally breached this essential principle.

On the morning of April 29, 1966, ZANU guerrilla units engaged Rhodesian regular forces in the Sinoia area.[23] They fought with courage that impressed even the Rhodesians. ZANU received much publicity in the international press. But the net gain for the revolution was nil. Men who could have been used more effectively within a revolutionary framework were killed or maimed. Others were arrested and thus lost for the revolution. On August 27, 1967 ZAPU guerrilla units, possibly wanting to upstage ZANU's Sinoia battle, engaged Rhodesian regular forces supported by South African forces and the Rhodesian Air Force at Wankie.[24] They fought with patriotic courage and inflicted casualties on the enemy, but again with little gain for the revolution. Throughout 1968 there were other such battles waged by ZANU or ZAPU guerrilla units against the Rhodesian regular forces.[25]

In early 1970 the desire for propaganda to boost the ZAPU image precipitated a crisis that fragmented not only ZAPU but also ZANU. James Chikerema, the vice-president of ZAPU and the leader of the party in exile, without consulting his colleagues invited a team from the British television program "Panorama" to film operations of ZAPU guerrilla fighters. Chikerema's colleagues were taken by surprise when the program appeared on British television stations. It is said the Zambian government was also angered by the fact that it had not been consulted, since some of the scenes that appeared were filmed on Zambian soil. A power crisis was precipitated in ZAPU as three senior ZAPU officials, led by J.Z. Moyo, sought to overthrow Chikerema. Gun battles were fought in Zambia between the two factions, and the Zambian government threatened to expel the whole ZAPU leadership from Zambia. Chikerema and George Nyandoro approached ZANU leaders with the idea of uniting ZAPU and ZANU, thus neutralizing the dissident ZAPU leaders. A crisis was precipitated in ZANU between those leaders who wanted unity with ZAPU and those who felt such unity would weaken ZANU. At one point it seemed as if Zimbabwe were going to have four parties in exile, each claiming to be the representative of the people. Then in 1971 one group of ZANU, led by Nathan Shamuyarira, and one group of ZAPU, led by James Chikerema, began to move towards unification. Shortly after this had begun, the other group of ZANU, led by Herbert Chitepo, and the other group of ZAPU, led by Jason Moyo, also began talking of unification. Shamuyarira and Chikerema united their groups into the Front for the Liberation of Zimbabwe (FROLIZ). Chitepo and Moyo did not merge their groups, but in 1972 they formed the ZANU-ZAPU Military Joint Command.

Zimbabweans have made their mistakes, and they will continue to make them. But they have learned from their mistakes. Both ZANU and ZAPU decided to take time for reflection and for re-examination of their strategies. Although the period between 1970 and 1972 brought frustrating experiences and internal conflicts to both ZANU and ZAPU, it was effectively used to prepare the people of Zimbabwe to assist the guerrillas and to resist regime pressure. While the two liberation movements between 1970 and 1972 were silently preparing the people in Zimbabwe to respond to guerrilla activities the regime and the white population became complacent, viewing the lack of open guerrilla activities as demonstrative proof that the guerrilla movements had been vanquished. The regime and its white population were taken by surprise when in December 1972 white farmers in Rhodesia fell victim of renewed guerrilla activity, and ever since the Smith regime has been deeply shaken by the continued attacks.

Recent guerrilla activities have demonstrated the maturity that the Zimbabwean liberation movements have attained. The operations are very different from the operations of the

1966–70 period. Charles Mohr of *The New York Times* reported on May 13, 1973, as follows:

> Black men are killing white men in this white-ruled southern African country.
>
> Groups of black nationalist guerrillas infiltrated into the northeast about the middle of last year and began living, moving and proselytizing among tribesmen.
>
> The Government of Prime Minister Ian D. Smith has conceded that it was not even aware of their presence for many months. Since December the guerrillas have been attacking lonely white farmers and clashing with security forces tracking them in the mountainous Miombo Forests and the tall grass of the bush.[26]

There has been evidence of increased support by the African masses for the guerrilla forces. The regime has attempted to destroy this support by imposing collective punishment on the African villages that support the guerrilla efforts. But such primitive measures have caused the African masses to identify themselves with the guerrilla movements. Allan Savory, a member of Parliament who resigned from the ruling Rhodesian Front, warned against these primitive measures. He said, "The Government simply panicked and is now antagonizing the local population by communal punishment which affects the innocent."[27] Reports coming from Rhodesia indicate that these measures have helped the personnel recruitment efforts of the guerrillas. Charles Mohr reported:

> More important, the guerrillas are following classical doctrine by placing heavy emphasis on political action and winning the support of people on tribal reserves. In the past they had seen less need for political action.
>
> There were probably only a few hundred infiltrators, but they have recruited some young men from the reserves who have joined in the attacks. *Outpost*, the magazine of the Rhodesian police, said recently that the guerrilla recruiting campaign was "intelligent, ruthless and efficiently carried out."[28]

Mistakes of the past have been used by the Zimbabwe liberation movements to guide them in the revolution. Emphasis is now being put not always on firing the gun but on prosecuting a revolution with an ideology, a revolution of revolutionaries, a revolution that maximizes the effects of every revolutionary act. However, when the revolution is being waged from an exile base, exile politics are bound to create obstacles to the revolution itself.

Exile Politics

There are two types of exiles from Zimbabwe. The first is the activist who operates the machinery of the Zimbabwe organizations in exile. Life in exile is fraught with endless frustrations, frictions, and fears. The frustrations are based mainly on the fact that the exiles are forced to carry out their politics away from home. Their contributions to the process of liberating their country tend to diminish, and as they fail to make an impact they must justify their own existence in exile. The exile must prove that he is away from home not because he is a coward, but because he is more effective in exile than he would be in the prisons of the oppressive regime. He must continue to show how effective he is, and he thus may be led to engage in certain activities only to prove to his hosts and to the world that his fighting capabilities have been improved in exile.

As the exiles meet with failure after failure in their political programs and as frustration piles on frustration, they begin to look for scapegoats. When they point fingers at each other, friction erupts among the exiles of the same political movement, further reducing the effectiveness of the movement. If these frictions are not quickly controlled or eliminated, splits occur as personalities compete with each other. Time and resources are wasted in trying to prove who is more representative of the masses at home.

Life in exile also depends to a large extent on the hospitality of the host country. Since the political movement in exile cannot get supporting resources from its own people at home, it is forced to depend on gifts and favors from foreign countries. The political movement has an axe held over its neck by the host and donor countries. At any time the host nation may ask the exiles to leave, or it may limit the type of military equipment that can be passed through the country because of security problems. Those countries that give assistance may reduce it or not send it regularly or cut if off completely. Thus the exiles live in constant fear. And no revolution can be prosecuted by fearful men.

Most political movements in exile find themselves faced with all these impediments. The revolutionary exiles of Zimbabwe have gone through these experiences, and most of them have begun to wish they had never left their country.

The second type of Zimbabwe exile is the student, who has gone or been sent abroad in search of the education said to be necessary for an independent Zimbabwe. When hope for a free Zimbabwe began to wane, some of these young people began to think of going to join the Zimbabwe political movements in exile. But most of these young Zimbabweans were against the type of revolution which was being prosecuted by ZANU and ZAPU. They were further disgusted by the way the ZANU and ZAPU leaders were treating the fighting men of Zimbabwe. A number of these fighting men had even fled to Europe to escape the treatment they were being subjected to by the leadership. They brought to the Zimbabweans already abroad frightening tales which discouraged many of them from going to participate actively in the political struggle. When in 1970 the leaders of ZANU and ZAPU began accusing each other of revolutionary deficiencies, these young people were further discouraged from joining the struggle. To keep alive politically they are members of the overseas branches of ZANU, ZAPU, and FROLIZ, but they too struggle with their own frictions, frustrations, and fears.

As the realignment of the Zimbabwe movements in exile

takes place, a new realization is occurring. The political exiles see that their host countries no longer tolerate them. They are being subjected to insults, humiliating procedures, and increased pressure. They have come to agree that there is no place better than home. But where is home? It is not where the Europeans of Rhodesia dehumanize the Africans of Zimbabwe but where the people of Zimbabwe can see their dreams come true. Such a Zimbabwe must be created by the Zimbabweans themselves. As the revolution is fought along the correct path, as personality conflicts are reduced, many young men and women of Zimbabwe now in exile will flock to contribute to the liberation of the motherland.

Political Opportunism

Every revolution has had to deal with the problem of political opportunism. There are people who side with the enemies of revolution for the gains they reap from such a relationship. Various methods have been used to deal with such men, from liquidating them to wooing them to disassociate themselves from the enemy and join the revolution. However, before a revolution decides what to do with opportunists, it must come to grips with the conditions that create opportunism.

Zimbabwe has had its share of political opportunists, but the way the Zimbabwe political movements sought to eliminate them did not contribute anything to the revolution. From the time of the formation of NDP in 1960 to the banning of ZANU and ZAPU in 1964, the Zimbabwe political movements sought to liquidate physically anyone who hobnobbed with the Rhodesian regimes. The main targets of the liquidation were the African chiefs and those Africans who supported the 1961 Constitution.

The chiefs were and still are on the payroll of the Rhodesian government and whoever pays the piper calls the tune. But the political movements of Zimbabwe never explained to the chiefs why they should not go on supporting the Rhodesian regimes; rather, they simply used violence to make the chiefs stop their relationship with the government. The more such violence was used, the more the chiefs were forced into the arms of the regimes. There is reason to believe—from the way the chiefs joined all other Zimbabweans during the Pearce Commission's survey in rejecting the 1971 Anglo-Rhodesian settlement—that if the Zimbabwe politicians had respectfully sought to explain the Zimbabwe cause to the chiefs they would have responded favorably. The chiefs are vital to the strategy of the Zimbabwe revolution. Africans respect authority and their elders, and the chiefs represent both. If they are won to the revolution, a large number of the rural people will be also. If they are alienated from the revolution, it will be difficult to marshall the support of the rural people. Therefore education, persuasion, and patient explanation of the realities of the Rhodesian situation must be used to convert the chiefs to the revolution.

There is another kind of Zimbabwe political opportunism which is more difficult to deal with. In 1962, although both NDP and ZAPU had declared that the African people would boycott the elections under the 1961 Constitution, forty-three Africans stood for elections to fill the fifteen "B" roll seats reserved for Africans in the Parliament of sixty-five. Of these forty-three African candidates, fifteen were unofficial Rhodesian Front candidates, fifteen others were United Federal Party candidates, and thirteen were Central Africa Party candidates.[29] All three parties were led and controlled by Europeans. In order for these African candidates to receive the support of their respective parties they had to capitulate to their platforms. In 1970 thirty-five African candidates stood for elections under the 1969 Rhodesian Constitution. They were competing for the eight elected seats which the Rhodesian regime had reserved for the Africans out of fifty-eight directly elected seats. If these Africans had the interests of the African people at heart they would not have emerged in such a large number to compete for only eight seats. They would have selected their best candidates, and the rest could have rallied behind them. But all these men had their eyes set on the $4,000 a year salary for a Rhodesian Member of Parliament. During the election campaign these candidates described each other as "playboys" and "money seekers."[30]

How should the revolution deal with such opportunists? Because of the infighting between ZANU and PCC in 1963 and 1964, the Africans resent the use of violence on fellow Africans. The revolution must ignore black opportunists, although the Rhodesian regime has dispatched all over the world the pictures of the black Members of Parliament, in an attempt to show that the African is participating in the Rhodesian political system.[31] These opportunists will gravitate to the stronger side.

International Dimensions

Although Rhodesia is a small country with less than six million people and is not of great economic importance, it has significance in international politics. It is important because a white minority regime is oppressing a black majority in an African country. Further, Rhodesia is a neighbor of South Africa and Mozambique, which are also ruled by white minority regimes in disregard of the aspirations of those who form the black majority.

It is necessary to understand the Rhodesian crisis from two angles. First, Rhodesia is a buffer state between the black majority ruled states of Africa and the white minority ruled territories of Africa. The Zambezi River, the northern boundary of Rhodesia, forms an ideological boundary between Pan-Africanism in the north and white supremacy in the south. Second, Rhodesia symbolizes the tacit connivance of the white world in the suppression of the black people. The economic and military resources used by Rhodesia to suppress the people of Zimbabwe are provided by the white world.

If Rhodesia falls to the people of Zimbabwe, South Africa will feel tremendously threatened by the forces of Pan-Africanism. When in 1967 Rhodesian regular forces seemed to be failing to contain the efforts of the African guerrilla units, South Africa did not hesitate to send its troops to assist the Rhodesian forces.[32] The African guerrillas received military and moral support from the Organization of African Unity and friendly African states. In Rhodesia the clash between white supremacy and Pan-Africanism is expressed through the alignment of support given to the principal adversaries.

This alignment of support has worked up to now to the disadvantage of the people of Zimbabwe. South Africa is a rich, developed country with enough economic and military resources to continue assisting the Rhodesians. It can afford to send its troops to foreign lands and still maintain security within South African borders. The African states which support Zimbabwe are newly independent, with weak economies, and susceptible to internal unrest, including military coups. Thus the support they can give to the Zimbabweans is limited. Although Zimbabweans know that justice is on their side and that they will win, the lack of economic and military support has forced them to wage their revolution with minimal resources. But what revolution was fought with plentiful resources?

Another international dimension of the Rhodesian problem is the support white Rhodesians receive from the white world. When in 1972 the Rhodesian regime detained Garfield Todd and his daughter Judy, there was an outcry all over the world. Britain even sent a special emissary to Rhodesia to investigate the situation of the Todds.[33] The white world had never made such an outcry when the Rhodesian regimes were detaining thousands of Africans, even when some of the Africans were shot and killed. Britain never sent a single emissary to Rhodesia to investigate the conditions and situations of the thousands of African detainees.

It has been shown in Chapter 5 how the white world assisted Rhodesia in overcoming the economic sanctions which Britain wanted the world to believe it had imposed against Rhodesia. An interesting point should be added to the story of this fiasco, illustrating how white people look at the oppression of black people by whites. When the United States Congress passed the Byrd Amendment, allowing American companies to import chrome from Rhodesia, it was stated that the USA should not import such a strategic commodity from the "non-free world."[34] Surprisingly, Rhodesia was part of the "free world," and the U.S. began to import chrome and nickel from Rhodesia. As long as it is the white people who oppress the black people Rhodesia will be called a "free" country by the white world. But let the case be reversed and one will hear cries of "oppression" and "communism."

The people of Zimbabwe must understand these international dimensions of the Rhodesian problem. Very often Zimbabwe leaders have behaved as if the white world will give them meaningful aid to overthrow a white regime. When they fly overseas they spend their time begging from white people and even entrusting some of the secrets of the revolution to some of their white "friends." They ignore the black constituency abroad. And yet it is the black people of the world who can adequately comprehend the plight of the people of Zimbabwe. They can become committed and effective supporters of the revolution. The white "friends" of some of the Zimbabwe leaders give a few thousand dollars to the revolution, but their economic enterprises give millions of dollars to the Rhodesian regime. The black people around the world may not have the finances needed for the revolution, but when the chips are down they will be dedicated supporters.

NOTES

1. Zambian *Daily Mail* (Lusaka), March 31, 1972.

2. *Ibid.*

3. *Rhodesian Parliamentary Debates*, vol. 71, Columns 879–80, July 18, 1968.

4. *Rhodesia Herald*, September 19, 1969. The Tangwena people were forced out of their homes in order for a European-owned ranch to be developed.

5. For details see Eshmael Mlambo, *Rhodesia: The Struggle for a Birth Right* (London: C. Hurst & Co., 1972), pp. 119–24.

6. See *Daily News* (Salisbury), November 1960-January 1961.

7. *Ibid.*, March 20, 1961.

8. Double Agent, "The Plot that Failed," *Central African Examiner*, August 1961.

9. F.M.G. Wilson, *Source Book of Parliamentary Elections and Referenda in Southern Rhodesia 1898-1962* (Salisbury: UCRH, 1963).

10. *Daily News* (Salisbury), April 13, 1962.

11. *Ibid.*, July 28, 1962.

12. *Ibid.*, February 9, 1962.

13. *Ibid.*, June 22, 1962.

14. ZANU, *Principles and Policies*, Salisbury, 1963.

15. Both Ndabaningi Sithole and Joshua Nkomo, the national leaders of ZANU and ZAPU respectively, have been in prison in Rhodesia since 1964.

16. Mlambo, *Rhodesia* p. 217.

17. *Rhodesia Herald* (Salisbury), June 23, 1966.

18. *Ibid.*

19. *Ibid.*, June 16, 1966.

20. *Ibid.*, June 8, 1966.

21. *Ibid.*, May 21, 1966.

22. *The Sunday Mail* (Salisbury), June 5, 1966, and the *Rhodesia Herald*, June 23, 1966.

23. *Rhodesia Herald*, June 7, 1966.

24. See Mlambo, *Rhodesia*, p. 215.

25. See *New York Times*, April 11, 1968.

26. *New York Times*, May 13, 1973.

27. *Ibid.*

28. *Ibid.*

29. "Southern Rhodesia Election—Candidates," *Central African Examiner*, December 1962.

30. *Rhodesia Herald*, April 3, 1970.

31. See *Rhodesia View Point* (Salisbury), March 1972.

32. *The Observer* (London), January 4, 1970. South Africa first sent 2,700 soldiers into Rhodesia and later increased them to 4,000.

33. Britain sent Philip Mansfield to Rhodesia to inquire into the situation of the Todds.

34. See USA Military Procurement Act 1971, Section 503.

CHAPTER 7

Six Requisites
for Revolution

For the revolution to succeed in Rhodesia six requisites must be met by Zimbabweans: (1) moral discipline, (2) development of a revolutionary ideology in conformity with Rhodesian realities, (3) coordination and trust between the leaders and the followers and among the leaders themselves, (4) prosecution of a silent revolution, (5) coalition of all struggling forces, and (6) sacrifice by all Zimbabweans.

Moral Discipline

Moral discipline involves adherence to principles that are not contradictory to the revolution. The revolution itself must set and enforce these principles. Although everyone involved in the revolution must discipline himself, the leaders especially must be beyond reproach. No one wants to fight a revolution so that his leaders may enjoy themselves after he has died for the motherland. No one wants to die to bolster the egos of his leaders and fatten their bank accounts in foreign capitals. Both the leaders and the followers must be instilled with the desire to fight for the motherland. They must be made aware that the interests of the nation are supreme.

Only men who can resist the tempations that surround the role of leadership can inspire their followers to persevere. Men who do in private what they condemn in public must not be given the chance to lead a revolution. Men with corrupt spirits, men who love wealth and cannot resist the temptations of life, cannot inspire their followers to lay down their lives for the motherland. A person who cannot put his own personal life in order, who cannot manage his own family, cannot be expected to lead a revolution. He should not be entrusted with the lives of dedicated men and women and the management of a nation in struggle.

Mere suspicion of the occurrence of acts contrary to revolutionary principles is sufficient to impede the revolution. Therefore the behavior of the revolutionary leaders must be such that no one within the revolution even suspects the existence of acts of corruption.

Even those who cling to corrupt personalities are guilty by default and association, for support of immoral leadership retards the revolution. Culpability also rests with those people within the revolution who propagate false rumors about the occurrence of acts of immorality and corruption in the revolution. The creation of rumors about the leaders very often leads to the demoralization of the fighters. Those who invent and propagate such lies are themselves enemies of the revolution.

Development of Revolutionary Ideology

As we have said in Chapter 6, the function of ideology in a revolution is to create a framework within which action is performed; it is a set of theories to guide actions.

The consequences of fighting a revolution without an ideology are many and disastrous, as we have seen. Action tends to be haphazard—forced on the revolution by expediency. Disputes easily erupt because there is no theoretical norm for action. And should a struggling people without ideology succeed in capturing political power, the tendency would be to maintain the same type of political, economic, and social policies as those of the overthrown regime. Thus in Zimbabwe, black masters and exploiters would fill the seats of the former white masters and exploiters.

A correct ideology for any revolution must emanate from the experiences of the people who are fighting it and must be in conformity with the realities of the country within which the revolution must be won. It must take into account the strengths and weaknesses of the enemy and of the people to be mobilized into the revolution. Applying a foreign ideology to a revolution is as disastrous as fighting a revolution without an ideology, because no ideology is tailor-made to suit all situations. However, this is not to say that a revolution should not utilize historical experiences of other struggling peoples. As Lenin put it, "What is required is the ability to treat these experiences critically and to test them independently."[1]

Along what path should the ideology of the Zimbabwe revolution be developed? First, it must be recognized that 80 percent of the Zimbabweans are peasants and only 20 percent can be included in the categories of the industrial proletariat and the bourgeoisie. Furthermore, in Zimbabwe there are very, very few African landlords.

It is fallacious to talk today of a class struggle in a Zimbabwe that does not have distinct classes, but it must be recognized that there is in existence a nucleus of a bourgeois-oriented African group. However, in Zimbabwe very few Africans are engaged in oppressing other Africans. Nearly all the African people of Zimbabwe are oppressed by the Rhodesian regime and by most, if not all, of the Europeans of Rhodesia. Therefore the Rhodesian conflict should not be viewed as a class struggle but mainly as a racial struggle. But if the revolution is waged without an ideology, classes will emerge in Zimbabwe after the racial struggle is won by the Africans. The revolution must be based on a theoretical

framework that will lead to the victory of the African people
and at the same time prevent the establishment of classes.
After the pains the Africans will suffer in the racial struggle
they must be spared the pains of a class struggle.

The ideology of the Zimbabwe revolution should serve
three functions. First, it must create a state of mind in the
Africans which will undermine the Rhodesian regime and the
white society. Second, it must present a blueprint for the
establishment of a just, man-centered society in Zimbabwe.
Third, it must provide an organizational framework within
which the revolution can be fought and won and which can
thereafter be adjusted to implement the blueprint for a just
society.

Of course the first function will be criticized as being racially oriented, but this should not bother the Zimbabwe revolutionaries. An ideology with racial overtones is in conformity with the experiences of the people of Zimbabwe and with
the realities of today's Rhodesia. This first function will be
self-terminating as soon as the white minority regime is overthrown. However, before such victory is attained the ills of
white-ruled Rhodesia must constantly be pointed out. Many
of these ills the African has come to live with and take for
granted. They must be constantly brought to the attention of
the African people and exploited to the maximum to raise the
political consciousness of the masses. A new state of mind that
refuses to tolerate oppression must be created.

This first function of the Zimbabwe ideology represents a
negative approach to the building of a nation. It calls for the
destruction of the political, economic, and social system of
Rhodesia. And yet it is necessary because the system that has
operated in Rhodesia for the past eighty-two years must unre-
servedly be destroyed. And it is the Africans who must destroy it.

The second function of the Zimbabwe ideology—to provide a blueprint for a just society—must put emphasis on the

Zimbabwe of tomorrow. The people of Zimbabwe can support the revolution only if their future living conditions will be better than what they are today. They must be assured that they will be able to recover their fertile lands, that there will be a fair land distribution, increased agricultural production, and fair marketing procedures. They must be assured of jobs, of education, of a fair return for their labor, and that the resources of the country will be used for the benefit of all and not in the interest of a few. They do not want merely to change masters. If the Africans are promised merely some vague better future they are not likely to join the revolution. They were promised by the ZAPU leadership in 1962 that African independence was "around the corner" and yet what was actually around the corner was the independence of white Rhodesia. They must be presented with positive and convincing ideas of how the ills of the Rhodesian society will be uprooted and the new Zimbabwe society will be built. It must be emphasized that only Zimbabweans can build the Zimbabwe they want.

There will be a small group of Africans who will feel threatened by an ideology centered around the peasant. Such a group will be interested in exploiting the peasants and living off them. Such people threaten to be the nucleus of a classist society in Zimbabwe. These Africans will oppose the development of a correct ideology and even encourage fighting a revolution without an ideology. They put emphasis on changing the faces of the rulers but not on changing the economic and social system of the country. However, if the revolution succeeds in capturing the minds of the masses it will be difficult for this small group to exploit others.

The third function of the Zimbabwe ideology is the creation of an organizational framework to fight and win the revolution and thereafter to rebuild the Zimbabwe society. Zimbabwe needs an organization of revolutionaries that enjoys the support of the peasants and the urban African residents. The organization will serve as the vanguard of the revolution. It should operate as an underground movement, and its membership must be restricted to the staunchest activists. Very few of the leaders should be known to the public, and the organization itself should operate in an atmosphere of mystery that promotes uncertainty and insecurity in Rhodesia.

Guided by the theoretical framework, the underground organization should tolerate and even encourage the establishment of a mass movement that operates in public and as much as possible plays by the rules of the Rhodesian regime so that it is not banned. This mass movement has as its first function the politicization of the people of Zimbabwe. If need be, it must claim disassociation with the underground organization, but in a way that will not discourage the people from supporting the revolutionary activities of the organization. In order for the two groups to work in harmony there must be coordination and trust among the leaders and between the leaders and the masses. The organization of revolutionaries cannot operate any effective programs without the people's support, but in order for the people to give such support they must first be politicized. Only a movement that operates publicly in Rhodesia, that provides visible leadership, can accelerate the politicization.

The mass movement must also realize that the struggle in Rhodesia can be won only through a violent revolution and that only an underground organization can lead such a revolution. Thus all who have the interest of Zimbabwe at heart will acknowledge the necessity of the existence of organizations that seem to be in contradiction with each other and yet are basically in harmony. To be able to acknowledge and accept such seeming contradictions Zimbabweans must have a theory for their revolution, an ideology that guides them through the contradictions. Friction and conflict between the mass public movement and the underground organization can be minimized only if a sound theory is developed.

Coordination and Trust

Between the leaders and the people. No revolution can succeed if the leaders are removed from the people. There must be continuous coordination between the leaders and the masses. When individuals are chosen to lead a struggling people they should not assume that they have power. They still belong to the oppressed people. It often happens among struggling people that individuals begin to behave as if they have been liberated as soon as they are made leaders. Zimbabwe has had its share of leaders who acted like prime ministers or cabinet members before the struggle was won.

If the revolution is to succeed there must be an end to an unapproachable leadership. Leaders must not be alienated from the people. The people must have trust in their leaders, and there must be feedback between the leaders and the people. No revolution can succeed if the leaders do not struggle side by side with their followers. This seems to have been the problem in Zimbabwe between 1960 and 1970. The leaders were aloof, unapproachable, and too "important" to struggle together with their people. Leaders must fight together with the followers and also die for the motherland. The revolution demands that any person not trained in guerrilla warfare and the art of revolution can never become a member of the revolutionary command. Only those willing to fight and die for the motherland should have the right to lead the revolution. After 1970 some leaders of the Zimbabwe revolution became willing to participate actively in the revolution, and thus progress has been made.

As the youths of Zimbabwe begin to trust their leaders and as they no longer feel that they are only the footstools of the leaders, more and more young men and women of Zimbabwe will join the revolution. These young people are the greatest resources of the revolution, and if they are mobilized into carrying their share the prospects of success are good. But they will be willing to carry their share only if the leaders carry theirs.

Among the leaders. Coordination and trust is also vital among the leaders themselves. Those who lead the mass movement must not be put into compromising situations by the claims of those who lead the underground organization. The movement's conditions of operation must be well understood by the underground organization. It is not easy to operate legally in Rhodesia. The leaders of the movement are likely to be under constant watch by the Rhodesian Secret Service. They may be forced to do things which the underground organization thinks should be condemned. Likewise, the leaders of the organization must not be put into situations in which they are compromised by the actions or statements of the leaders of the movement. The leaders of the movement must not alienate the masses of the people from the leaders of the armed struggle. The leaders of both parts of the Zimbabwe struggle must not sacrifice long-term gains for the sake of short-term or propagandistic victories.

It will not be easy for the two groups to operate in harmony because of the different stresses and strains each is subjected to. But if there is trust and coordination the effectiveness of each can be maximized. The problem, however, is to establish the coordination in such a way that the movement is not banned. Should the regime detect coordination between the mass movement and the underground organization it will ban the movement. The leaders of the regime might decide to exploit the strain that is bound to exist between the two elements of the revolution. In fact the Smith regime has been arresting able men around Bishop Muzorewa, the leader of the African National Council. The regime's strategy is to isolate the bishop and then to entice him into denouncing guerrilla movements of Zimbabwe with the hope that he can arrive at a "genuine" arrangement with the regime under which the lives of the Africans can be "improved." Such an arrangement would of course worsen the strains between the leaders of the two elements.

However, Zimbabweans must find ways of maintaining visible leadership and a public machinery for the politicization of the people. The announced aim of this movement need not be the overthrow of the regime by force. It is enough to emphasize the need for maintaining visible leadership and a machinery for politicization. Zimbabweans must not be frightened by contradictions. All revolutions have had to encompass them, and only those that mobilized the contradictions of their situation to serve the revolution have succeeded. In his celebrated essay "What is to be Done?" Lenin wrote, "Only those who are not sure of themselves can fear to enter into temporary alliances even with unreliable people; not a single political party could exist without such alliances."[2] Zimbabweans should ponder this. But the alliance must definitely not be with the Rhodesian regime, because in such an alliance the African will be the victim.

The Prosecution of a Silent Revolution

The problem of unsought publicity.   When one looks at what has happened in the Zimbabwe struggle one can only regret much of the publicity that the revolution has received. Some has been forced on the Zimbabweans, and some has been the product of the Zimbabweans themselves.

The scarcity of resources with which the Zimbabweans fight their revolution has forced them to ask friendly nations for resources. The Organization of African Unity (OAU) is the chief provider for the revolutions that are being waged in Southern Africa. The OAU receives its resources from African states and other friendly states and organizations. Two problems arise. First, many African states have used their support of the liberation struggles in Southern Africa as publicity for their own foreign policies. They publicly announce the support they intend to give to the OAU Liberation Committee for use in the liberation of Southern Africa. A number of the states make known in detail the amount of their support and the channels through which it is sent. But after they have announced and pledged their support they often do not follow it through. The regimes in southern Africa, however, take these claims of support from African states very seriously. They prepare themselves to fight liberation movements which seem to be receiving support from forty-one independent African states plus other states and organizations. They do not take into account the fact that the claims of support often do not materialize. Thus the revolution suffers not only from lack of resources or deficient resources but from the psychological impact such claims make on the enemy. The claims raise the state of preparedness of the enemy without raising that of the revolutionaries.

At other times the support of certain African and non-African states does materialize, but the military hardware given to the liberation movements is of a World War I or World War II vintage. Very often the liberation movements have found themselves fighting with guns that do not fire. They have lost men because of defects in the equipment. The Southern African regimes of South Africa, Rhodesia, Mozambique, and Angola, however, are very often equipped with the most modern weapons from Britain, France, West Germany, and the United States.

There is, however, some genuine support of the revolution of Zimbabwe, and the Zimbabweans are grateful for it. Those who aid the Zimbabwe revolution do not have the obligation to do so. They give aid mainly because they sympathize with the plight of the Zimbabweans and want to see justice triumph.

The second problem posed for the revolution by reliance on OAU aid arises from the stipulation of the OAU Liberation Committee that such aid can be given only after the liberation movements have put their plans of action before the Committee. There are seventeen African states represented on the

OAU Liberation Committee; the Committee has to report to the OAU Council of Ministers which has a representative from every African state; in turn the Council has to report to the OAU Assembly of Heads of State. The OAU bodies are not known for keeping secrets. In fact within the OAU there are states which hobnob with the regimes of Southern Africa. Thus by the time the liberation movements launch their plans, the regimes already know what is coming.

As long as the revolution relies on aid from friends and sympathizers these problems will continue to plague it. It can only be hoped that the Zimbabwe revolution becomes strong enough to capture weapons from the regime's forces. Without such weapons it seems the revolution will have no resources to continue fighting, but the revolution needs at least some initial resources in order to capture these weapons. Success can come only if this vicious circle is broken.

The problem of sought publicity. The Zimbabweans themselves have at times sought publicity—not to strengthen the revolution but for its psychological benefit. The desire to justify their own existence in exile and to seem to be fighting effectively against the regime forced ZANU and ZAPU between 1966 and 1969 to claim victories that did not occur. Propaganda is an instrument of war which can be very effective, but its effectiveness depends on the ability of those who use it to maintain some sort of credibility. When an organization predicts that targets will be hit, and then fails to hit them, this reduces its credibility. Later, if the organization succeeds, the public will refuse to believe its claims. Even when the effects of the successful operations are visible, the regime can claim that accidents or natural causes were the source of the damage; if on previous occasions they have been substantiated, the regime's claims would tend to be believed by the international public.

The desire of both ZANU and ZAPU to reap propaganda value from the operations of their forces between 1966 and

1969 frequently led to their sending men to fight in Zimbabwe at inopportune times. If one examines the pattern of operations of the Zimbabwe forces, especially in 1968 and 1969, one notes that very often forces were sent to fight at the time the OAU bodies were about to meet. The parties wanted some gunfire to back their claims at the OAU conferences. Very little was achieved by such propaganda strategies. Men were lost, and the OAU did not significantly increase resources allocated for Zimbabwe.

As we have seen, it was the desire for publicity to boost ZAPU's image in 1970 that precipitated the fragmentations of both ZANU and ZAPU. Although these fragmentations have led to healthy and effective discussions by the Zimbabweans, the lesson should not be forgotten: the desire for publicity nearly destroyed the parties of Zimbabwe in exile; it nearly alienated the Zambian government, which has been one of the staunchest supporters of the liberation of Southern Africa; and no direct gains were achieved by such propaganda moves.

What is needed in Zimbabwe is the prosecution of a silent revolution by men whose faces are not known to the general public. Let the operations of the revolution speak for themselves. The activities of the guerrilla forces since December 1972 have been very conspicuous to the world, and the regime itself has been forced to admit these successes. The regime has been providing the publicity for the guerrilla activities.

However, for there to be a silent revolution two things must be done. First, there must be a coalition of all the fighting forces of Zimbabwe. This will reduce competition and thereby eliminate claims designed to outmaneuver the other elements. Second, the revolution must depend primarily on Zimbabwean resources. This will reduce the need to claim successes in order to pressure friendly states and organizations into giving aid to the revolution.

There is much to be gained from a silent revolution. The trickling of revolutionary secrets to the regime and its friends can be reduced; friction among the leaders can be controlled;

and an atmosphere of mystery that is essential for a revolution can be fostered, thereby creating panic and psychological disorder in the supporters of the Rhodesian regime.

Coalition of All Struggling Forces

Zimbabweans must begin to examine why since 1963 the elements of the Zimbabwe struggle have not come together to form a national front to spearhead the revolution. In 1971 the Zimbabweans in the motherland buried their differences and united in the African National Council, which successfully led to the African rejection of the Anglo-Rhodesian Proposals. And yet in the same year Zimbabwe parties in exile which could have formed one underground organization were polarized and plagued with splits that led to the formation of FROLIZ and the continued existence of ZANU and ZAPU as separate entities. Why can the parties in exile not follow the example of the Zimbabweans in the motherland and form a national front? The ANC represents the mass movement; after they have established underground cells in Zimbabwe, the parties in exile can truly lead the armed struggle.

At no time in Zimbabwe has the split of the political movement been on the basis of ideology, since the various groups in the struggle have not had an ideology until very recently. Furthermore, although the Shona and the Ndebele tribes have historically had their differences, tribalism has never been predominant in Zimbabwe. ZANU and ZAPU were never split on a tribal basis until the polarization of both parties in 1970, when it can be said that tribalism became a factor. Joshua Nkomo, the national leader of ZAPU, is a Kalanga and identifies himself with the Ndebele; yet the majority of his executive council and of his followers were Shona. Ndabaningi Sithole, the national leader of ZANU, speaks Ndebele more fluently than he speaks Shona and on his executive council there were men, like Enose Nkala, who were not Shonas. Here and there a few individuals with frustrated

hopes have appealed to tribal feelings, even dividing the
Shona tribe into its dialectic composition as a basis of political
organization. They have tried to establish tribal bureaucracies
to promote their personal interests.

The major cause of splits in Zimbabwe politics is personality. Leaders who have eyes on the future government of Zimbabwe have competed for power even though such power is
not in sight. Some of the leaders seem to believe that they
were anointed by God to lead the Zimbabwe nation and have
resisted the emergence of new leaders.

There is much to be gained by uniting the Zimbabwe
forces. The resources of the revolution are limited and cannot
be spread thinly. As long as there are two or more revolutionary parties the Rhodesian regime's opportunities of recruiting
informers continues to increase. Many young men and women
who want to join the revolution will continue to shy away
from active participation because they do not want to be en-
tangled in personality politics. But nothing should divide patriots when the nation is in danger, when the honor of the
motherland lies trampled by an immigrant minority group.

Sacrifice for Zimbabweans

The sight of Zimbabwe leaders flying from one foreign
capital to another begging for money is humiliating to a proud
people. If all Zimbabweans within and outside the motherland were to contribute to the revolution, at least maintenance
resources for the revolution could be found. But before people
sacrifice their lives and resources they must be convinced that
such sacrifices are not in vain. If the revolution of Zimbabwe
is goal-oriented and not personality-oriented there is no doubt
that Zimbabweans will rally around forces that are united for
the revolution.

No one will ever come to liberate Zimbabwe for the Zimbabweans; the Zimbabweans must do this for themselves.
They must provide both the human and the material resources

to fight the revolution. They must be willing to sacrifice their lives and all they have, for no revolution was ever won without sacrifice by the people.

NOTES

1. V.I. Lenin, *What Is to Be Done?* (New York, International Publishers, 1972), p. 26.

2. *Ibid.*, p. 18.

Postscript

The International Expectations of Zimbabweans

Zimbabweans do not want sympathy from the world; they only want their cause to be understood and the difficulties of their situation to be appreciated. Those who give assistance to the regime of Rhodesia must know that they are assisting in the oppression of a people. Zimbabweans demand that the assistance which is being given by the white world to the Rhodesian regime to prop its oppressive system be terminated. Zimbabweans further expect that whatever the fate of the white men should be in Zimbabwe, the white world should refrain from interfering.

From the non-white world Zimbabweans expect a deeper understanding of the problems they face in their revolution; when the chips are down Zimbabweans expect the non-white world to restrain the white world from interfering in the affairs of Zimbabwe.

From all people who cherish freedom and human dignity, Zimbabweans ask for material assistance—not simply for themselves but for the sake of justice.

Rhodesia has arrived at the crossroads in its political development. Lines of confrontation are clearly drawn. The less that international involvement props up an evil regime the sooner justice will be established. Zimbabweans are fearful that as events begin to tip in their favor some foreign powers, especially Britain with the assistance of her allies, will intervene to "maintain law and order." Such intervention would cause an outright race war, not only in Rhodesia but in the whole of southern Africa. Zimbabweans expect world opinion to restrain those who will urge such intervention. Law and order in Rhodesia was broken down by the Rhodesian regime in 1965. And since then Rhodesia has been a lawless society. Thus the pretext of foreign intervention in Rhodesia on behalf of "law and order" when the Africans are assured of victory should not deceive world opinion.

Furthermore, world opinion must guard against being presented with a scheme for a Rhodesian settlement couched in catchy terms like "multi-racial settlement." One needs to look at the colonial history of Britain. The British are noted for working out political schemes that allow them to withdraw from the scene or to wash their hands of the problem, after which the schemes collapse. One needs to look at the Middle East problem, at the Cyprus problem, at the Nigerian crisis, at the Bangladesh crisis, at the South African problems. In each of these crises Britain was the colonial power that withdrew, leaving a settlement that collapsed a few years after.

Britain will give its blessings to a Rhodesian scheme accepted by the so-called Rhodesian European "moderates" and the African "moderates." It will sell this scheme to the United Nations and the world. A test of acceptability for any scheme should be whether it allows the masses of the people to participate in controlling their own destiny, in managing and even mismanaging their affairs. Any scheme that falls short of this element of justice will lead to bloodshed. The Zimbabwe people expect all people who cherish freedom and justice not to support a scheme that does not give justice to the masses of the people.

As the armed struggle of Zimbabwe scores some successes the Rhodesian regime will begin, as it has already done, to point at those who fight for their country as terrorists eager to liquidate white people. But the liberation movements of Zimbabwe do not use terror in their activities. It is true to say a number of European civilians have fallen victims of the activities of Freedom Fighters. But in each incident there was a reason that led the Freedom Fighters to perform the acts. Terror involves indiscriminate killing. The Freedom Fighters of Zimbabwe do not use indiscriminate killing as an instrument of fighting a revolution.

Let us look at one incident which occurred in 1973. An armed Freedom Fighter entered a European-owned store in northeast Rhodesia. He saw a European woman and her three young children. He told the woman that he does not fight against women and children and then left. The woman telephoned the police, who came heavily armed. The Freedom Fighter was located not very far from the area. He was outnumbered, but the regime's police did not even try to arrest him. They just gunned him down. Who was the terrorist in this incident?

It is now on public record that on December 16, 1972 Rhodesian troops assisted Portuguese soldiers in mass murders of at least four hundred unarmed villagers in Mozambique. This is indiscriminate killing. Women and children, old people and sick people were killed in Mozambique by both Portuguese and Rhodesian troops (*Washington Post*, July 15, 1973). This is terrorism. It would therefore seem that it is not the Freedom Fighters that are terrorists but the regime's troops and police. Terrorism does not occur only when the victims are white. It occurs also when the victims are non-white—the color of a person's skin does not make one life worth more than the other, although some people have tended to behave as if non-white people are expendable.

Zimbabweans expect world opinion to regard them as people who are fighting for freedom, for justice and dignity, and not as terrorists. World opinion must care as much about black people who are victims of white injustice as it has always cared about white people who are victimized by blacks. Rhodesia is going to provide the test of fairness to a world that speaks so much of justice.

APPENDIX

Proclamation Broadcast by
Ian Smith on November 11, 1965

Whereas, in the course of human affairs, history has shown that it may become necessary for a people to dissolve the political affiliations which have connected them with another people and to assume among other nations the separate and equal status to which they are entitled, and

Whereas, in such event, a respect for opinions of mankind requires them to declare to other nations the causes which impel them to assume full responsibility for their own affairs,

Now therefore, we the Government of Rhodesia, do hereby declare:

That it is an indisputable and accepted historic fact that since 1923 the Governments of Rhodesia have exercised the powers of self-government and have been responsible for the progress, development, and welfare of their people.

That the people of Rhodesia, having demonstrated their loyalty to the Crown and to their kith and kin in the United Kingdom and elsewhere throughout two world wars and having been prepared to shed their blood and give their substance in what they believed to be a mutual interest of freedom-loving people, now see all that they have cherished about to be shattered on the rocks of expediency.

That the people of Rhodesia have witnessed a process which is destructive of those very aspects upon which civilization in a primitive country has been built, they have seen the principles of Western Democracy and responsible government and moral standards crumble elsewhere; nevertheless they have remained steadfast.

That the people of Rhodesia fully support the request of

their Government for sovereign independence and have witnessed the consistent refusal of the Government of the United Kingdom to accede to their entreaties.

That the Governments of the United Kingdom have thus demonstrated that they are not prepared to grant sovereign independence to Rhodesia on terms acceptable to the people of Rhodesia, thereby persisting in maintaining an unwarrantable jurisdiction over Rhodesia, obstructing laws and treaties with other States in the conduct of affairs with other nations and refusal of assent to necessary laws to the public good, all this to the detriment of the future peace, prosperity and good government of Rhodesia.

That the Governments of Rhodesia have for a long period patiently and in good faith negotiated with the Governments of the United Kingdom for the removal of the remaining limitations placed upon them for the grant of sovereign independence.

That in the belief that procrastination and delay strike and injure the very life of the nation, the Government of Rhodesia considers it essential that Rhodesia should obtain without delay sovereign independence, the justice of which is beyond question.

Now therefore, we the Government of Rhodesia, in humble submission to Almighty God, who controls the destiny of nations, conscious that the people of Rhodesia have always shown unswerving loyalty and devotion to Her Majesty the Queen and earnestly praying that we the people of Rhodesia will not be hindered in our determination to continue exercising our undoubted right to demonstrate the same loyalty and devotion in seeking to promote the common good so that the dignity and freedom of all men may be assured, do by this proclamation adopt, enact and give to the people of Rhodesia the Constitution annexed hereto.

God save the Queen!

SOUTHERN AFRICA

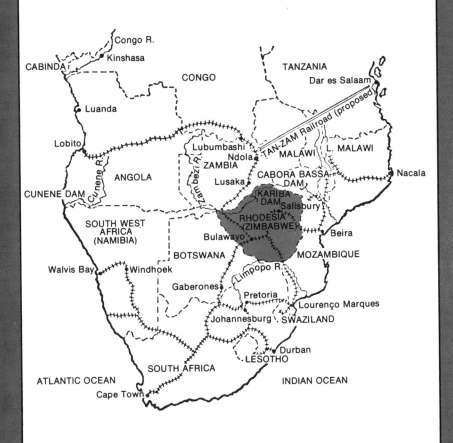

++++++ major railroads

Reproduced from *International Affairs*
Vol. 47, No. 1, January 1971, p 21.

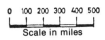

Scale in miles

Index

Abraham, D.P., 2

Africans: attitudes towards Europeans, 8; brutality of, 6-8; children of, 7; distrust of, 5-6; religion of, 81-82; voting of, 75

African Nationalists, 47

African National Congress, the (ANC), also African National Council, 8, 116, 123, 125, 126, 133, 156, 161

agricultural rights, 4

American Potash and Chemical Corporation, 77

Anglican Church, see churches

Anglo-Rhodesian Proposed Settlement, 97, 107, 113, 115, 144, 161

armaments, 158

Beadle, Sir Hugh, 32, 45

Beadle Tribunal, 32

Botswana, 68-69

Britain, membership in, 2, 5

British South Africa Co. (BSAC), 4

Bulawayo, 8

Burrough, Bishop Paul, 97, 100

Carter Report, 28

Catholic Church, see churches

Cecil Square, 5

Charter Company Justice, 8

Charter Law, also Charter Ro, 8

children, 7-8

Chikerema, James, 125, 135, 138

Chitepo, Herbert, 135-138, 171

chrome, export of, 77

Christian influences, see churches

churches: Anglican, 82, 86, 88, 94, 97, 100; Catholic, 82-84, 86-87, 90, 92-96, 98, 100-101, 103-104; Christian Council of Churches of Rhodesia, 91-92, 97, 100; Dutch Reformed, 82; educational contribution of, 84-87, 94-96, 122-123; Methodist, 80, 82, 86, 88, 95, 99, 103; missionary efforts, 82-84; political influence of, 84, 90, 94-96, 100-104; Salvation Army, 82

coal, 66

colonialism, 118

Commonwealth Fact Sheets, 18

Kane, Nora S., 6
Kaunda, Kenneth, 71-72

Lamont, Bishop Donal R., 90, 103-104
Land Apportionment Act, 29-30, 34-35, 45, 90, 94-97, 101, 122, 125
Land Husbandry Act, 29, 101, 122, 125-126
Land Tenure Act, 14-16, 29, 94-95, 100, 102, 122
Law and Order (Maintenance) Act, 59
Lendy, Capt. Charles, 7
Liberal Party, origins of, 30
Limpolo River, 2
Lippert Concession, 4
Lippert, E., 2, 4
Lobengula, 2, 5

Macguire, Rochfort, 4
Malawi (see also Nyasaland), 65-67, 69-70
Mashona, 1-2, 8
Mashonaland, 6
Matebele, 2-3
Matebele War, 5
Matebeleland, 5-6
Mawena, Michael, 33, 126, 128, 130
Methodist Church, see churches
mineral rights, 4
missionary efforts, 82-84
Moffat, Rev. John, 2-3
Morris Carter Commission, 28
Muzorewa, Bishop Abel, 88-89, 156

National Democratic Party (NDP), 33, 123, 126, 127-130, 143
Native Land Husbandry Act, 16, 29
natural resources: chrome, 77; coal, 66; copper, 66; diamonds, 2; oil, 68
Ndebele Monarchy, 5
Nkomo, Joshua, 125-131, 134
Nyasaland (see also Malawi), 38-39
Nyerere, Julius, 65

Occupation Day (see also Pioneer Day), 7-8
Organization of African Unity (OAU), 65, 135, 146, 157-160
oil, 68